CLEAN
SWEEP

Also by Peter West and published by W.H. Allen

FLANNELLED FOOL AND MUDDIED OAF

Jack.
Thanks for your company
+ good cheer.
Peter West

CLEAN SWEEP

Peter West

W.H. ALLEN · LONDON
1987

Copyright © Peter West, 1987

Typeset by Phoenix Photosetting Chatham
for the Publishers, W.H.Allen & Co. Plc
Printed and bound in Great Britain by
Mackays of Chatham Ltd, Chatham, Kent
44 Hill Street, London W1X 8LB

ISBN 0 491 03347 8

PREFACE

This is a cricketer's diary of an unexpected journey and, I hope, an acceptable day by day account for cricketers of a happy and remarkably successful expedition. It is mostly, though by no means all, about what happened on the field of play – or what I thought might happen.

It was a joy to tour with a team well managed and well led. I thank all the players for their good cheer and friendly disposition to an ageing scribe. I thank my media colleagues for making me feel so welcome.

I am also very grateful to *The Daily Telegraph*, and to its editor, Mr Max Hastings, for enabling me – quite out of the blue – to fulfil a lifetime's ambition by reporting an England cricket tour. I am also greatly indebted, as an early page or two will reveal, to an old friend and rugby colleague who first prompted the idea that by hiring this reporter the paper could tide itself over a temporary difficulty occasioned by the resignation of their cricket correspondent.

I wish I could say that my subsequent relationship with the management of its sports desk was always a happy one. I found it disheartening to be told only twice, in the course of a tour lasting four months, that it had quite liked something I had written. A donkey offered carrots so rarely had to sustain himself with the hope that his readers overall were satisfied.

Photographs courtesy of: *All-Sport/Adrian Murrell* (1, 3, 4, 5, 7, 8, 9, 11, 17, 23, 24) *Patrick Eagar* (2, 6, 10, 12, 14, 15, 16) *John Woodcock* (18, 19, 20, 21, 22)

CLEAN SWEEP

August 21 1986

This diary of an unexpected pilgrimage starts here. Third Test, England v. New Zealand, at The Oval: my last for BBC television. The game ends for everyone except the Kiwis on a frustrating, watery note, and for me on rather an emotive one when I am chatted up by my old colleague, Brian Johnston, on Test Match Special, and then on TV.

Michael Austin, not Mike Carey, has been writing the leading cricket reports in *The Daily Telegraph* for perhaps a fortnight. I have assumed that Carey was indisposed. But at a Cornhill lunch I learn from David Grice, sports editor of *The Sunday Telegraph*, that Carey has resigned. It appears that when Imran Khan suffered racial abuse from some white yobbo during the Worcestershire-Sussex NatWest semi-final, Carey was just about the only reporter not to mention the fact. Sports editor, Radford Barrett, apparently not best pleased. Acrimonious telephone conversation, as I read it, ensues. I am not privy to its details, but for Carey, who may have suggested that he had been sent to cover the cricket and *not* extraneous matters, I suspect that a long-running battle had come to its end. He must have blown his top.

I am surprised to hear from David Grice the names of several successors to Carey now being optimistically paraded at *The Telegraph*.

1

August 25

Telephone call from John Reason, erstwhile rugby correspondent of *The Daily Telegraph* but for some years likewise
on the *Sunday*'s books: a forthright, fearless writer, the
most widely read in the rugby world, whose columns,
whether you agree with them or not, are compulsive stuff.
John, who has always been concerned for the well-being of
everything at Peterborough Court, sounds much concerned about developments. He says that the latest solution proposed is that Tony Lewis, who will be in Australia
covering the first three Test matches for *The Sunday Telegraph*, should be asked to provide a similar service for the
Daily, and that E. W. Swanton, who has thrown his hat into
the ring, would report the last two. This sounds a perfectly
sound idea to me but it appears that Jim, now in his 80th
year, is thought to be too old. Yet he is marvellously well
preserved, and I would cheerfully back him to deliver the
goods in his best old style.

Then comes an inspired piece of thinking by 'J.R.' 'What
the paper needs,' he says, 'is someone with a bit of a name,
like yourself, to tide them over the winter. Do you have any
objection if I suggest it to Ted Barrett?' Having contem-
plated a relatively quiet hibernation in the Cotswolds, and
now, as a free-lance always committed to winter rugby at
home, foreseeing unlikely visions of a lifelong ambition
being fulfilled, I say: 'What a splendid notion, J.R.' I am
then obliged to report the conversation to my wife, Pauline,
who I like to think was expecting to see rather more of the
breadwinner during the coming months. 'The odds,' I said,
'must be at least 20 to 1 against, but in the event of a miracle,
can I go?' I thank the good Lord for an ever-supportive,
understanding better half.

August 28

It so happens that I have long been pledged to give Ted
Barrett lunch today. I have agreed with John Reason that I

will know nothing about his telephone conversation with me, nor about a subsequent one with Ted which apparently began unpromisingly but finished with the penny dropping in an encouraging fashion. Within ten minutes I get a tentative enquiry about my future movements and within two more I am offered the job, subject to approval of the new editor, Max Hastings. I return home walking on cloud nine, ring J.R. to congratulate him on his perspicacity and a piece of salesmanship superbly done, and dash off a letter to Michael Austin, who, I know, desperately wanted to go on the tour himself. Pray God he believes me when I tell him that this is not of my making.

September 5

I am wheeled in to meet the newly-appointed editor, Max Hastings, who confirms everything and leaves his sports editor to sort out the nitty-gritty. I have to be careful not to admit that I would happily go for expenses only. Sports editor subsequently mentions a fee which I say sounds rather mean, and we settle on the figure he probably had in mind in the first place.

This evening, BBC TV sport, inspired by my cricket producer, Nick Hunter, give me a marvellous farewell party, hosted by Cliff Morgan with charismatic flair and generosity, and attended by many old friends and colleagues including dear old Rex Alston, now 85, who gave me my first radio cricket broadcast in 1947. He had his obituary notice printed by *The Times* last autumn, and has just married for a second time. Life in the old dog yet.

September 6

The NatWest final, Lancashire v. Sussex: my very last match for Beeb television, and another 'oldie', Clive Lloyd, probably making his final bow, too. Clive gets a rapturous welcome walking out to bat, makes a rapid 0, and loses. I do

3

much better, NatWest giving me a gold medal inscribed to 'P.W., a man of many matches'. Although TV has overshot its scheduled time, Nick Hunter keeps the broadcast going until I receive it. There are still some nice, thoughtful people in this world, not least Glen Emanuel of NatWest. For me, a moment to savour.

September 8

Still one hurdle to cross, since I am verbally pledged to cover rugby regularly for HTV Bristol this coming winter, as well as helping to put together a documentary about the great Walter Hammond. I present a *cri de coeur* to their director of programmes, Ron Evans. 'Don't be a BF,' he says. 'Of course you must go to Australia. Come back and do the rugby when the cricket's finished.' A terrific gesture from someone now my friend for life.

September 14

Our 40th wedding anniversary, and a super party, cunningly staged for Darby and Joan who expect to see a few relatives at the home of their elder son, Simon, and are met with a cast list of about 50 – old friends including Les Ames, who had come all the way from Canterbury to Bath, Tom Graveney, Clem Thomas (Wales and British Lions) and Bill Knight, a former British Davis Cup player of immense grit. Our younger son, Stephen, makes a felicitous address. For once I am left virtually speechless. Blessings bountiful on Simon and Valerie, Stephen and Sheila. The only sad thing in a lovely day is that our daughter, Jackie, and Will are away in Cyprus with their two children, Nancy and Dan.

September 27

It is proposed by the *Telegraph* that I send messages from Australia on one of these new-fangled computers. I am therefore summoned to Fleet Street for a crash course in operating a 'Tandy'. To one almost incapable of mending a fuse the whole thing seems a baffling mystery, but I take the infernal gadget back home and promise to practice on it. Not before I have bumped into Michael Austin, who assures me that he harbours no personal ill will. I get a different reception from my supposed friend, John Mason, rugby correspondent. 'You've heard,' I say, 'that I'm going to Australia?' A rather pregnant silence and a distinctly cool look. 'Yes,' he replies. 'Very surprising, and very disappointing.' Well, I can't expect the staff lads to rejoice, and I mustn't lose any sleep over it.

October 11

Mike Gatting's braves flew off to Australia two evenings past. Now comes the day for this intrepid reporter, in cricket touring terms with an L plate on his back. I have produced an exhaustive list of jobs still to be done in the garden, and packed far more clothes than I suspect I shall ever need. Sheila drives us to Heathrow so that the parting will be a little easier, and my wife Paul will have company on the way back. I have been away from home many, many times over the last 40 years but never for more than four or five weeks. This will be a four-month separation, although Paul will be coming out for the final Test, in Sydney in January, and staying over until the end of the tour. How much less daunting it is for someone setting off to witness new things, meet new people, and rise, if he can, to new challenges. The one left behind is faced with all the old familiar routines. More lonesome, too, when the family has long since fled the nest. But she has all our children and grandchildren close at hand, and I know they will do their stuff.

It is a British Airways flight to Auckland, via Bombay, Perth and Brisbane, and I am grateful to the *Telegraph* for allowing me to go in 'Club' class. Anything for greater comfort on a trans-world trip, which is exciting the first time you do it but an awful bore thereafter. I listen dutifully to

advice that passengers can ameliorate the effects of jet lag
by not partaking of alcohol but work myself into a good stu-
por at BA's expense and sleep most of the way to Bombay.
This is my third visit to India, and just like the first two: a
refuelling stop at an airport. Disembarking briefly at Perth
with Paul Weaver (*Daily Mirror*), I find the night temperature in early Australian spring rather less inviting than the
ones left behind in an Indian summer of mists and mellow
fruitfulness. And so on to Brisbane, mid-morning and 85F
under a cloudless sky. I was last in this city, with the
England rugby team, in 1975. No Ashes battle will be more
fiercely fought than the one between England and Australia at Ballymore here. It started with a fearful fracas and
only sobered down after Mike Burton had left, as Eddie
Waring was wont to say, for an early bath.

October 13

What a lovely sensation, disembarking in Brisbane, to feel
the sunny glow on a balding pate. Temperature at 10.30
hours in the 80s, but after all it's still early spring. I check in
at the team's hotel, the Mayfair Crest International, which
at once turns out to offer excellent service with a constant
smile. The natives are certainly friendly. I meet up with
those journalists who flew out with the team: Ted Corbett
(*Star*), Martin Johnson (*Independent*), Chris Lander (*Sun*),
David Lloyd (Press Association), Graham Otway (*Today*)
and Graham Morris (free-lance photographer). Johnson
and Lloyd, like me, are on their first cricket tour.

I miss the team's second net practice, held in the morning, and inquire of Martin Johnson what news is cooking.
'The Aussie press tell me,' he replies, 'that if Ian Botham
farts, the news hounds will come flying out from home.'
Then, remembering the status of his new paper, he added:
'I think they might have said "breaking wind".' In fact,
things are very quiet indeed. The manager, Peter Lush, has
very sensibly decreed that he himself, Micky Stewart, assis-

6

tant manager in charge of pure cricketing matters, and the captain, Mike Gatting, are alone empowered to talk officially to the media. This, at one good middled stroke, has got the press boys off the big man's back, and it seems clear already that a relaxed I.B. is enjoying the experience.

October 14

What a good net session at the Anglican Church Grammar School. Excellent surfaces: firm, fast and true. Stewart pushes the lads hard, and Botham, in a long, impressive stint of bowling, produces his old outswinger again. My word, if he can resurrect that weapon from his armoury, it's exciting news. I later ask a weary I.B. whether he thinks Micky Stewart will be planning two nets again tomorrow. 'I fucking well hope not!' he replies with a grin. I then record a 'progress report' piece in a radio interview with Mike Gatting, having pledged myself with the BBC to be the poor man's Henry Blofeld until he arrives later in the week. Dinner with the Middlesex duo, John Emburey (vice-captain) and Philippe Henri Edmonds, who tells me that Australia has already sold 8,000 copies of his wife's best-selling *Another Bloody Tour*, and that she is shortly on her way out to promote it further. Is there any place in the world with better sea food than Brisbane?

October 15

It is clear that Micky Stewart is running his ship on a tight but ever cheerful note. For variation, today he ordains a game in the middle. Some of the younger scribes are recruited to help in the field, and Chris Lander distinguishes himself with a fine, running catch at third man. I report this for my newspaper but doubt that they will print it. I can't see the *Sun* and *Telegraph* in rivalry for customers, but editorial desks can be meanly parochial. I preface my piece by saying that the only hot news from this sun-drenched city is that there isn't any. A good job, too. Nice to concentrate on the cricket alone, and watch the form at the nets. Reporters for the 'pops', who can be enterprising and even inventive at such times, must be scratching about to keep their editors happy.

Arrival of John Thicknesse, an Harrovian representing the London *Standard*, and of 'Blowers', an Etonian representing, so far as I can make out, pretty well everybody. The last named is very big news in Australia, where he is regarded as being the archetypal plummy English Pom. Like Brian Johnston, another Etonian, he is eternally, unrepentantly his own man. I should think he makes a fortune dashing off radio interviews on the hour, making commercials for Channel 9 and writing thousands of lively, controversial words for what seems like half the newspapers in this country. Enough, anyway, to enable him to give me a splendidly generous dinner at the Sheraton, where the waitresses seem willing simply to prostrate themselves in the great man's presence. A lovely surprise at that hotel is to meet Diana Fisher, wife of Humphrey Fisher, an old friend and television colleague long since working for ABC in Sydney. Of 'Dizzy Di' there is bound to be more anon.

October 17

Enough of net preparation: to the first match, at Bundaberg, 250 miles north-east of Brisbane, close to the southern end of the Great Barrier Reef where, the travel brochures excitingly inform us, we may languish on the coral sands and fossick all day. No chance, alas, of a fossick for the moment.

We fly in a Fokker Friendship aircraft over Queensland's orange groves and cattle ranches to what is locally described as the fourth best climate in the world. Languishing by the motel pool in a gentle zephyr under a cloudless sky, I wonder how splendid the top three must be.

Bundaberg, with its rich alluvial river flats, is a nurseryman's paradise known as a verdant salad bowl. The district also produces one fifth of Australia's sugar cane, a greater share of the nation's rum and more tomatoes than anywhere else, not to mention exotic delights such as avocados, aloe vera, macadamias, lychees, granadillas, custard apples, sousop, guava and paw paw. At one day-lily centre you can take your pick from 600 named varieties, some of quite staggering beauty and delicacy. The Queensland king fern, rising to 18 feet, is said to have the largest fronds in the world. There are cacti, some of them 100 years old, and a ravishing range of gerberas (like our dahlias) as well as acacia, callistemon, casuarina and eucalyptus.

October 18 (first day v. Queensland Country XI)

First day of the first encounter, against Queensland Country XI, on a cricket Oval with a flat pitch smoothed by a motor roller driven by a groundsman who is a dead ringer for our own Test umpire, David Shepherd. Even in early spring, he needs a canopy to protect him from the hot sunshine. Not something we're likely to see at Lord's. England make 491 for 4. In spite of a throat/chest infection Mike Gatting, a merciless destroyer of any bowling short of the highest class, thrashes it round and out of the park for 171. Ian Botham, emerging 25 minutes from stumps, in stygian gloom forlorn, strikes 51 not out off 25 balls. 'Six, six, six' chant the local lads, and the hero obliges next ball. An astonishing performance. Chris Broad (97), Wilf Slack (70) and Bill Athey (73 not out) miss the headlines but all three play well. Athey looks polished, immaculate. Slack loves the feel of a bat in his hand, and has a serene temperament. Broad uses his height to stand up and strike the ball, short or well pitched up, productively off his legs. But he runs out of early gas and is dropped twice. The show could hardly be off to a better start, but what does it mean, against country opposition?

October 19 (second day v. Queensland Country XI)

Heavy rain overnight, and when I say heavy, I mean it. The pitch survives but even the Bundaberg outfield can't dry out quickly enough to allow play before lunch. Running out of time, Gatting declares, and the Country XI finish on 149 for 6. We bowl with no great distinction against some good, old-fashioned English names: Schulte and the brothers Scuderi. There is a violent storm soon after play finishes. 'Doesn't look too good for the morning,' I say to my taxi driver. 'Don't worry. You'll be right, mate.'

October 20 (third day v. Queensland Country XI)

We weren't. A very sticky, oppressive day, and another late start. England soon get the last four Country wickets (Phillip DeFreitas 3 for 10 in 5 overs), then Gatting decides to bat again. So much for his assertion at the start of it all that he would do his best to win every game. It is made to sound a very hollow bromide. But all captains tend to be the same when it suits their book to change course. The game expires after a second token declaration by the Country captain, Bruce French batting through for 63 not out, playing some handsome off side shots and needing plenty of luck.

October 21

Back to Brisbane. Letter from assistant Sportsed enclosing cutting of story back home and telling me that I have missed it. The story holds that Ian Botham may after all earn cash for extramural activities, manager Peter Lush having backtracked on previous decision. The fact is that I.B. – and all other players – have been free from outset of tour to do just that, provided such activities don't impinge on the cricket. I suggest to assistant Sportsed that story was cleverly concocted at a time when nothing much was happening and inquire if I had been sent out here to write fiction? The big thing today is the launch of Jeff Thomson's biography, *Thommo Declares!*, which is hailed on the reverse of its jacket as encapsulating 'the deeds of the fastest, most feared and often the most resented bowler in the history of cricket'. It is written by an Australian journalist, John Byrell, whose previous masterpieces have included some short stories under the intriguing title of *Down The Loo*. Mr Byrell prefaces each chapter with some thoughts from his subject. One of them, under the heading 'Those **!?@¢!!*+@! POMS!', goes as follows: 'I dunno. Maybe it's that tally-ho lads attitude. You know, there'll always be an England and all that Empire crap they dish out. But I never could cop Poms . . . generally speaking, that is. As soon as they lobbed here in '74, I couldn't wait to have a crack at 'em. I thought "Stuff that stiff upper lip crap". Let's see how stiff it is when it's split!' The author's style is not dissimilar. 'Letting rip at around 90 mph, Thommo gave the startled English the lot – short kickers, careering outswingers, screeching wides, full tosses, blockholers, straight low screamers.' You'd never believe from all this that Thommo is a down-the-middle, modest bloke.

Before the *Thommo* launch I watch another net session which confirms my confidence that Phillip DeFreitas, at 20 the youngest member of this side, will soon be winning his first Test cap. With his high, whippy action he is getting as much bounce as anyone out here and, in the middle, hitting the keeper's gloves with an encouraging thwack.

No one, not even the natives, seems to know the location of Lawes, where we are due to play another country match tomorrow. There is a theory that because England insisted that it should not be played more than 60 miles out of Brisbane, someone shut his eyes and put a pin in the map. None of the Brisbane taxi drivers, all of them willing conversationalists, can help. 'Must be a one-horse town, mate. But you might have trouble finding the horse.'

I enjoy nice ziz by the pool on the top, 16th floor of the Mayfair Crest International, which has a splendid view of sky-scraping city centre by the wide and winding Brisbane river. I have read somewhere that Brisbane's first inhabitants were convicts established in a penal settlement in 1824. With its rapid development in recent decades it has become an extraordinary mixture of the Victorian/Edwardian and the concrete/glasshouse. It is a brash, cheerful, outgoing place. Everyone seems very friendly and helpful.

Some scribes and players go off to the golf course. I wish a wonky back did not stop me from getting such good exercise. Back then to the pool for some gentle swimming. Must do something to keep weight down. Have no plans to ration intake of quite splendid Australian wines.

October 22

'Gatt', 'Both' and 'Thommo' go deep sea fishing, and 'Both' impresses the local pundits by hauling in a sail-fish, weighing 72 lbs, which goes to the taxidermist for proof and preservation of another of his spectacular catches. It took him an hour, using a light line. Rest of party proceeds by coach to mysterious Lawes, which we find is the 2,500-acres estate of Queensland Agricultural College. It is a lovely day on a fine ground set against distant azure hills. Vibrant crowd come from far and wide, most of them in bush hats. Foster's and XXXX do roaring trade. The 'piggery' end emits easily identifiable odours, and the flies do good business too. I circle the Oval with 'Blowers', instantly recognised and chatted up by almost everybody. I feel I ought to be holding up the king's train. Chris Lander wears a 'Mount Gay' sun-cap, which seems an unfortunate choice for one of such relentlessly orthodox proclivities.

October 24 (first day v. Queensland)

I remember reading, when I was a lad, about the old Woolloongabba ground in Brisbane, and how the pitch was levelled by a horse-drawn roller. These days it is a splendid modern arena; not too large, not too small. To the right of the scoreboard, jacarandas still in springtime glory and, behind them, still to bloom, the poincianas. At the far, Stanley Street end, a long stand, hot sun glistening on its concrete forecourt, named after Clem Jones, a former mayor of Brisbane who, as curator here in 1974/75, produced a pitch on which Lillee and Thomson caused the greatest apprehension in English ranks. Further to the left, the weeping fig trees. The field itself, almost circular in shape, is surrounded by a dog track, but it is grass, not dirt, and lush at that. So the prospect does not jar.

George Tribe, a very fine left arm leg-break and googly bowler who played long ago for Northants., turns up while on holiday from Victoria. So does Andrew Slack, captain of the grand-slam Wallabies rugby team in the UK in 1984/85 and, much more recently, of their team which won a series in New Zealand. To win in the land of the Kiwis takes a lot of doing. It has left Australia cock of the rugby union walk. Slack has been an underrated centre, though not by the players. A delightful man, now stockbroker-cum-journalist.

So much for the good news. Starting the serious business of the tour, a four-day State game against Queensland, England win the toss and are bowled out for 135. Gatting top scores with a rugged 35, Emburey has to be prised out, French battles away for 11 undefeated. But both openers, Broad and Slack, depart for very few, Gower looks as if he is batting on borrowed time, Lamb and Botham are dismissed through lack of application or judgement. After this horrendous beginning England are looking down the barrel, and Queensland, 52 for no wicket off 35 overs at the close, are in no hurry to squeeze the trigger.

October 25 (second day v. Queensland)

We miss four chances during a Queensland opening partnership of 154, and I observe two of them, appropriately enough, from under those weeping fig trees. After all that,

England do pretty well to get seven men out on a peach of a pitch 'ere Border declares at 311 for 7. The persistently unflagging Small, a very genial character, has the best figures (3 for 60) but DeFreitas looks the sharpest, most penetrating of the pace quartet until he is given a few overs too many. In the last twenty minutes Slack, who was out for 1 in the first innings to a good ball, gets an even better one – an outswinger he has to play – and falls to a blinding low catch. It can be a hard old game.

October 26 (third day v. Queensland)

Encouraging recovery to 339 all out after four gone for very few and another brief, exotic innings from Gower, who looks like a millionaire anxious to cash in at the bank. What is his attitude on this expedition? In the space of four months he has lost the captaincy both of England and Leicestershire, has not been appointed vice-captain out here, or even asked to be one of the selectors. So he has no official status. He is clearly finding it very difficult to keep nose to grindstone. However, Lamb, exuding bubbling confidence, makes 65, Botham strikes a rousing 86, young DeFreitas makes 20-odd and Foster, who fancies himself as a batsman, finishes with 74 not out. But by stumps Queensland are well on the road to victory.

October 27 (fourth day v. Queensland)

Greg Ritchie makes a vigorous 50 and we lose by 5 wickets shortly after lunch. Then the rain sets in. Temperature a wretched 64F. What a penance a reporter's life can be.

But the big story today, not a new one because Chris Lander had it in the *Sun* a long time ago, is that Ian Botham is making his last England tour. He confirms it at a media conference and announces that he plans henceforth to spend roughly six months in England, six months in Australia, where he will, subject to official approval, play for Queensland. Who can blame him? He and his family will love the life out here. He is a natural beachcomber, but he won't need to doss down on the strand. He has an impressive Australian agent, Tom Byron, who will ensure him more than a decent living. He is just as big news here as he is at home. He should be a riot at the Gabba. I report to my newspaper that, so long as his form demands it, he must continue to be picked for England Test teams at home. He can continue as a batsman of world stature for years yet, if he has the inclination.

October 28

Flight to Wudinna via Sydney/Adelaide, the first leg in a Boeing 767 apparently fashioned in steerage class for thin people with very short legs. Pre-Christmas, we are due to see a lot of Sydney airport where the weather now is just like home: sullen and wet. The 727 to Adelaide is more comfortable, England's captain continuing to while away the hours by playing picquet with John Thicknesse, and the vice-captain likewise with Graham Otway, known as 'Otters'. We are offered a Vino a Pirramimma Cabernet Sauvignon 1984 which features 'a clear bouquet of freshly crushed berries and "dusty" oak, plus a hint of herbs and violets'. It might have done had it not been brought out of the fridge.

The terrain beneath now looks redder, much drier. We fly the last leg to Wudinna in a twin-prop Short 360, its final descent and a good old buffeting in high winds not being to everyone's liking. Mike Gatting might have been brave enough after a bloodied, re-shaped nose in the Caribbean to return there for further shelling from the West Indian batteries, but he now abandons the picquet and looks distinctly apprehensive. Bill Athey looks so queasy he has to recline on the Wudinna tarmac and then take to his bed, so missing an immensely friendly local reception in the evening. The manager, Peter Lush, is as sick as he was when given five 'good tips' for the Brisbane races, none of them finishing in the first three.

Aforesaid reception is addressed by 'Blowers', being a late stand-in for Mike Coward of the *Sydney Morning Herald*, who is said to be a very amusing and polished performer. 'Blowers', a natural Thespian, holds court for well over half an hour with immense panache and clearly loves every minute of it. He has just given the England team a fearful bashing on the air and in his syndicated Australian column, and is not one whit abashed to answer questions from the audience in their presence.

Wudinna is in the South Australian wheat and barley belt, about 400 miles north-west of Adelaide across the Yorke peninsula. An hour's drive from the Great Australian Bight, it offers vistas of grain silos and distant plains. The locals say they can't get television unless the wind is blowing in the right direction. This may mean that 'Blowers' will get rather less than his royal welcome when he circles the ground tomorrow.

October 29 (one-day match v. South Australian Country XI)

A heavy black clay pitch got its last roll under floodlights at midnight. The presence of England here is the biggest thing since invention of sliced bread. No doubt it is a good thing to be showing the flag, but the exercise is totally irrelevant in terms of serious cricket. England win by 9 wickets against very modest opposition, Broad and Slack making further 50s, frustrated only by the flies who have started their new season in rustic parts with relentless enthusiasm.

The flight back to Adelaide is placid. We book in at the Hilton International, its outward concrete horrors belying sybaritic comforts within.

October 30

It is a gentle, 20-minute stroll to the cricket ground along wide, tree-lined streets at whose traffic lights, when the red light says 'Don't walk', a prudent man pays heed. If you don't get booked by a copper for jay-walking, you may easily be run down by traffic moving very fast indeed.

If the Adelaide Oval is not the most beautiful cricket ground in the world, it can have few rivals for the title. Port of Spain in Trinidad perhaps. Newlands in Cape Town? The river Torrens, winding through public gardens fresh in springtime radiance, gives its name to the southern end. In the mid-distance, a backcloth of the blueish Mount Lofty ranges. At the northern (St Peter's Cathedral) end, the most stylish of big Australian-type scoreboards is so tastefully framed between the weeping fig trees that it is classified by the Australian National Trust.

There are grassy banks at both ends, and on one side a long stand with a reddish roof. The Oval is green, elegant and largely unchanging. It has the longest straight boundary of any ground in the world: 110 yards from wicket to gauze sightscreen, which is something to put even Ian Botham on his mettle. This is the ground where Bill Woodfull was struck over the heart, and Bert Oldfield hit on the head (off a top edge), by Harold Larwood in 1932/33, when the Bodyline series came to boiling-point. I am told there were some 50,000 spectators that day, most of them standing. The capacity now is upwards of 30,000 – comfortably more than that of any English Test arena.

Pat Gibson (*Daily Express*) has arrived to join the scribes, without looking at all happy in his work. Gloomy exterior may mask a wryly humorous nature.

October 31 (first day v. South Australia)

We have had word from home that the *Star* has reacted to the latest Botham story with the miserable, green-eyed headline 'Good riddance!' Green-eyed because Botham is the *Sun's* man.

Gatting loses the toss on the first day of the game against South Australia, who make 305 for 8 – rather better for England than at one time was feared. Wayne Phillips, dashing Test left-hander but no longer Australia's wicket-keeper, hits 116. Emburey and Edmonds do a lot of good bowling.

I dine with Peter Lush as guest of 'Blowers' at the Adelaide Club, where his choice of wines is impeccable and the whole aura is one of restful, old-fashioned comfort. The secretary there is Major Brian Gardner, an outstanding all-round athlete in his days at St Lawrence School, Ramsgate, who was my opposite number at stand-off half when I played my last game for Cranbrook. 'You ran round me with some ease,' he recalls, becoming my friend for life.

November 1 (second day v. South Australia)

South Australia's skipper, David Hookes, declares at the overnight score and we have another gruesome start: Broad lbw 0, Athey a hairy 18, Gatting out for 8 to a good catch but a chancy shot. In first-class innings to date Broad has made 7, 18 and 0, Slack 0 and 1, Athey 18. Oh dear, who the hell opens in the Test match? Broad has certainly looked good in the country games.

Lamb, still exuding great confidence, happily makes 105, and James Whitaker, in his first big innings in Australia, contributes an impressive 108. The young Leicestershire batsman hits the ball hard with a rather rigid method: short back lift and not much follow-through. He seems to have a very sensible head on his shoulders and realises that he needs to be patient. No obvious place for him in the Test side with Gower, Lamb, Gatting and Botham listed at Nos. 3 to 6. Not yet, anyway. But England were 38 for 3 when he came in, so it was a fine effort.

We are later treated to another splendidly responsible

innings by Botham, who makes 70 off 62 balls with ten 4s and, for once, no 6s. It is 382 for 8 at the close.

I have talked in the press box with the great 'Tiger' O'Reilly, now rising 81 and still writing unfailingly trenchant columns in the *Sydney Morning Herald*. 'I first met you,' he says, 'on the Don's tour of England in 1948.' Not a bad memory.

Walking round the ground with 'Blowers', I am asked for my first autograph in Australia. He doesn't get a touch. I chalk it up as a definite success. This has been the day of the traditional Adelaide pageant, an hour-long procession of floats with Father Christmas bringing up the rear. Yuletide starts early out here.

November 2 (third day v. South Australia)

Winning position attained. Dilley and Edmonds whack another 25 for a first innings lead of 103. On an extremely docile pitch we then get them 84 for 3. Phillips (70) and Hookes dominate the afternoon but Emburey takes 5 wickets in succession for a score at stumps of 261 for 8 – a lead of only 158. Edmonds takes two fine catches but gets no wickets. Not a day when the quick bowlers are queueing to get on: Botham has just 6 overs.

There is a point in time when the Middlesex triumvirate of Gatting, Emburey and Edmonds fiddle with their field settings while 12th men come and go with helmets, shin pads and heaven knows what else. Sleep, the State side's leg-spinner, is batting on a dozey pitch. Progress soporific. But we are poised for the first important victory of the tour, even though we can't blot out of our minds the memory of three opening stands worth 14, 4 and 1. If misfortune continues in this regard, would England consider using Whitaker to open? He has had some experience of it in his days with Leicestershire 2nd XI. I ventilate the little thought in the *Telegraph*.

November 3 (fourth day v. South Australia)

The last day of the State game is a scorcher: 90F in the shade, and ton-up plus elsewhere. Alas, Athey fails again, though hearts should bleed as he is picked up by the keeper off an authentic but too thin leg glance. But Broad scores an impressive 63 with some sweetly timed strokes. I think that in all fairness to Slack he must get another chance against Western Australia in Perth, otherwise his tour will be slipping right away from him.

A century partnership between Broad and Lamb ensures England's first success, outside one-day contests, since they beat Jamaica last February. The final margin should have been more conclusive but some flippant shots are played. Attentive Botham and faithful Emburey restore order, doing a favour to those of us intent on catching the 6 p.m. train. Victory by 5 wickets.

It was Graham Otway's idea to make the old-fashioned journey to Kalgoorlie, but in the end he can't manage it himself. 'Blowers' and I leap at the thought of something different from another of those 32 internal air flights. David Gower and Phil Edmonds join us, and so do Scyld Berry (*Observer*) and Adrian Murrell (a director of *All Sport Photographic*). 'Blowers' works on his contacts in high places, and half of the Australian rail hierarchy insist on adding a special coach and giving us a champagne send-off which delays departure by 30 minutes. Did E. W. Swanton ever get better treatment in his finest hour? The only snag I discover is that 'Blowers' and West have been stupid enough to pay for their tickets, and everyone else is on a 'freebee'. You win some and you lose some.

Darkness soon falls over the South Australian plain and its stock pastures. But we all have a very convivial dinner and, fortified by many Cognacs, I can't remember hitting the pillow.

November 4

I awake at 6.30 to blue skies and a breakfast of which British Rail would not have been ashamed. After fourteen hours, *still* in South Australia, we reach the unchanging flat landscape of the limestone Nullarbor plain. The curvature of the earth's surface on a restricted horizon gives one the same sort of sensation as being at sea. Mile upon mile, as they say, of bugger all. It takes me some time to remember my classical education. *Nul arbor*. Never a tree in sight; for 500 miles ant hills are the only undulations.

The Indian–Pacific is one of the great railway journeys of the world. Our train started from Sydney on Sunday. We boarded it on Monday evening. It will arrive in Perth, some 2,500 miles away, two mornings later.

Still in South Australia, we arrive to stretch legs briefly at Cook, where the diesel engine and carriages are refuelled/rewatered. It boasts a population of about 100, all on railway or telecom duties, and two prison huts, carefully preserved, in which old criminals were contained before being moved to something larger. We seize on postcards at the souvenir stall proclaiming, 'If you're crook, come to Cook. Our hospital needs help. Get sick.'

Here on the Nullarbor the line stretches dead straight for a world record 297 miles, which is not far short of the distance from London to Edinburgh. Snooze off, wake up and the vista outside is arid and unchanging: mile upon mile of salt and blue bush, myall, mulga, mallee and myoporum. Occasionally, we espy kangaroos, who must be pushed to scratch a living. Eventually, we churn past a sign which says 'Welcome to Western Australia' and, much later, we observe a tree again.

We arrive in Kalgoorlie on time, and book in to another of those bath-less Australian motels where the ripe odours of bacon, fried eggs, sausages and steaks pervade the entire ambience at breakfast. It has been a good trip; something I wouldn't willingly have missed.

November 5 (one-day match v. Western Australia Country XI)

Another glorious Australian springtime day, and another very comfortable victory over modest opposition. England 293 for 5 from 50 overs; Western Australia Country XI 176 for 9. Wilf Slack and James Whitaker each get all but 50, David Gower continues his rake's progress (36), and Bill Athey, who can't go wrong in our one-day contests, follows up an elegant 124 with 3 wickets. He has no rival for the man of the match award.

A matutinal taxi tour, with John Thicknesse, gives us sight of the mine where gold was first struck in 1893 and of the Hay Street red light district, Kalgoorlie's answer to Hamburg's Reeperbahn and the Zeedyk in Amsterdam. The ladies are not permitted to stand outside, toting for business, until the children have gone home from school. By the end of the 1960s some of the mines here were no longer worked, but gold now fetches such a price on world markets that our taxi driver says: 'Anyone who can't make a good living here, mate, simply isn't interested in work.'

The media is more than well catered for at the cricket. Drinks are brought to our tables. Oysters and prawns are served for lunch. How much more generous the Australians are to visiting reporters than we are to theirs. I am not forgetting that Cornhill treat them decently at home Test matches.

November 6

Our first day in Perth. The Ambassador hotel offers spacious, comfortable quarters but is sub-standard in almost every other respect. Indignant messages are soon being sent to the lady at Kuoni in London, Margaret McConnel, who has done a splendid job for us so far but had clearly been unable to book us in at something better because of the influx of visitors for the seemingly eternal America's Cup bonanza. The Ambassador, alas, soon makes a big blunder indeed.

Bill Rumsam is a big, bluff north Devonian builder-cum-farmer who, having ostensibly made an adequate pile, must be spending something like £25,000 on following the tour from A to Z. He has been a genial companion for the press gang. Now, on the day we all arrive in Perth, a telex is sent from home with the grievous tidings that his mother has died of a heart attack. The hotel sit on that telex for many hours.

To a happier topic: a walk to the Western Australian Cricket Association ground (known as the WACA) through public gardens with lily pools and black swans, and oleanders, bouganvilleas, hydrangeas and marigolds all in colourful bloom. The WACA is ringed now by four great concrete pylons topped, so it is claimed locally, by the best floodlights in Australia.

The square, totally re-laid some 15 months ago, does not yet produce the pace and bounce of yesteryear, but is still thought to be the sort of surface on which Australia plan to make early inroads in the Test series. All the pitches have been slightly re-angled to permit a better view from a new members' stand. It is now all but a very fine modern arena. How infinitely superior Australian Test grounds are, in general appearance and amenities, to those at home.

At England net practice, we have first sight of Christopher Martin-Jenkins, the BBC's very professional cricket correspondent, Alan Lee (*Mail on Sunday*), David Norrie (*News of the World* – an old rugby colleague of mine) and Mark Austin, who has transferred his allegiance from news coverage for BBC television to the opposition. I must not forget to add that Matthew Engel (*Guardian*) joined up with us in Kalgoorlie. The doyen, John Woodcock of *The Times*, is now expected to adorn our company when we return to Brisbane for the first Test, having recovered from his back troubles. Tony Lewis (*Sunday Telegraph*) likewise – without such problems. Robin Marlar (*Sunday Times*) is expected to fly out for Tests three, four and five and in the meantime, Peter Roebuck, captain of Somerset, will deputise for him with a very talented touch. Somerset's skipper cannot leave home until after certain domestic matters have been resolved at a special general meeting shortly to be staged in Shepton Mallet. But we already seem to have enough men at our disposal to field about two teams, all of them, I dare say, more confident about how matters should be handled in the middle than those who actually have to conduct them.

We have been wondering what to write about on a quiet day when the Australian selectors do us a favour with an unexpectedly early announcement of their 12-man squad for the Brisbane Test. Geoff Lawson has been recalled to the colours. No surprises in batting line-up, which is wearing a more settled look than for some time, notably after a short tour of India which produced a tied match in Madras and two draws. The two left arm over the wicket bowlers, Bruce Reid and Chris Matthews, will soon be inspected by England here. Matthews has yet to play in a Test. Greg Matthews is the only Australian specialist spinner named. I compose some thoughts sitting in blissful sunshine close to those black swans, with the WACA towers astride the trees. But the locals have dire concern about a very serious week-end drought: workers at the Black Swan brewery are threatening a strike.

November 7 (first day v. Western Australia)

First day against Western Australia, a very hot one indeed. England put the home side in and bowl them out for 275. It should have been a lot less. Three catches and several half chances are spilled, the clearest being one off the bowling of DeFreitas that went twixt Lamb and Gower in the slips – Lamb looking closer to it – when Chris Matthews had made a single. Matthews, a rugged customer, no duffer with the bat, then carves 56 off 57 balls and adds 84 with Marsh, Australia's Test opener, who makes a chanceless hundred. We bowl pretty well on an even-tempered pitch, DeFreitas

24

having 4 for 82 and Botham 3 for 41. For the last over of the day it is Gladstone Small, not Wilf Slack, who emerges as Chris Broad's partner. A thoughtful gesture on the captain's part, Slack having made 1 and 0 against Queensland, but not one suggesting that Gatting had too much confidence hereabouts in one of his accredited openers. A nightwatchman to *open*? When did that last happen, short of injury or illness?

In the evening, we find that a local paper is running a front-page story (apparently paraded in the *Sunday People* back home) about Ian Botham upsetting British Airways stewardesses on the flight out to Australia by walking about in his underpants and requesting to see their knickers. Peter Lush scotches such lurid stuff with the remark that in his view, this piece of journalism had sunk to the very bottom.

November 8 (second day v. Western Australia)

A rather dramatic and unexpected change in the weather. 90F forecast again, but Perth plunges, à la Melbourne, 30 degrees lower. We awake to lightning and claps of unseasonable thunder. Less than half an hour's play. Small soon departs, the ball swinging and cutting about. Broad and Slack not at all reluctant to accept offer from umpires in bad light.

During a break before play is finally abandoned for the day, Messrs. Thicknesse and West challenge captain and vice-captain to a game of bridge. 'Thickers' is obviously a very good player, and keenly competitive, too. 'Embers' brings to his calling a sense of adventure not so apparent when he is wheeling away in the middle and, with two productive 'doubles', I foresee a handy source of income should it rain regularly in the future.

Still no letters from my wife, Paul, but there are postal problems in the Gloucester area and none of those she has written has yet got through to me. One got as far as Adelaide the day we left that fair city, and was promptly posted back to her. She tells me on the 'phone – thank God for one efficient service – that she has lately been feeling lonely and depressed but that the family are being wonderfully supportive.

A most pleasant evening chez Ken Casellas, cricket reporter for the *Western Australian*, and his wife, Pam. It is his 50th birthday, as we later discover. All of the press gang are invited. Ken is a keen gardener and I am able to admire his blaze of roses and petunias.

November 9 (third day v. Western Australia)

The news is through to us that Somerset's committee have won their case at the special general meeting; departure of Viv Richards and Joel Garner thus confirmed. The focus now on Ian Botham and his predictable reactions. If there is any surprise at the press conference he conducts at the Sheraton hotel, it can only lie in the vehemence, even bitterness, with which he reaffirms his intention to quit the county. 'I suggest Peter Roebuck stays in London,' he says. 'He'd be a lot safer.'

I report to my paper that I am relieved to know that the Somerset committee have won such a handsome vote of confidence, which must strengthen their resolve to rebuild their side and end an era of 'player power'. I regret that Somerset's supporters should now be denied regular sight of a Titan of a cricketer who has put loyalty to Richards and Garner above his allegiance to a club which, I suspect, has stood by him in his bad times just as he has served them well in the good ones. 'Blood is thicker than water,' he says.

Whither Botham now? Worcestershire are said to be front runners to sign him up, but not before the new year. Bowlers may blanch at the prospect of coping with Botham and Graeme Hick on a bland pitch. Botham ends his conference with the words: 'I am on my last tour. I'm going out on a high. I hope the Australians know what's coming.'

Not for the moment, perhaps. It is, alas, a third day of a

match when England slump to 69 for 6 before Botham, going in at No. 8, gets his head down yet again to make 48. We are bowled out for 151. Bruce Reid, a gangling 6ft. 8ins., destroys the cream of our batting, Chris Matthews sweeps away the tail. Matthews reminds me in run-up and action of John Dye, erstwhile of Kent and Northants. Am much impressed by Ken Macleay, who bowls medium right arm, close to the stumps, with a nice high action and movement either way. He would prosper in England.

At the end of a dire day England are no nearer to resolving their biggest problems. Who opens in the Test? One has to be Broad, who gets 33 today, but he does look vulnerable around his off stump. Slack (15) has now failed three times. Athey? I think it must be him. Gower, second ball, is bowled by an inswinging yorker which I think he lost sight of. Genuinely bowled out on this occasion, but there is less excuse for others. Gatting plugs away circumspectly for one and a half hours, happy to see Botham going firmly, before being bowled by Matthews. For a batsman of his gifts, the England captain *does* get his castle knocked over rather often.

Dinner at their lovely home with Dr David and Ann Haultain. David is long time president of the West Australian Rugby Union. As a former Scottish referee, he was the touch judge when Andy Hancock's spectacular try robbed Scotland of a deserved victory at Twickenham in 1965. He likes to say that Herbert Waddell, doyen of the Scottish hierarchy, has never spoken to him since because he was convinced that Hancock put a foot into touch. Our son, Stephen, did a locum for David on his way back from an obstetrical year in Auckland in 1980, and told me afterwards that his host kept an excellent cellar. Now I am able to confirm the fact.

I met Frances Edmonds in the press box today. She has been in Australia for some time, promoting her best-selling *Another Bloody Tour*. Philippe tells me it has sold 50,000 copies in England already. I find her very lively and stimulating company. An ungallant colleague suggests that a little goes a long way.

November 10 (fourth day v. Western Australia)

The home captain, Graeme Wood, declares his second innings leaving England notionally to get 331 at 5-plus an over. Not an adventurous decision. Perhaps he thought four hours long enough to bowl England out again. If he did, he looks to have it right for a while, for we witness another woeful batting display.

Five for 2, Slack and Gower gone for 0, the last-named collecting a pair and now paying a price, I think, for his lack of time in the middle. Gatting also makes 0. Broad gets 25 but he is still looking a bit fallible outside his off stump. Lamb rattles up a good 63, Richards contributes a useful 17 and Botham, ever with nose to grindstone, makes 40 not out as a drawn match is ensured. It is not a result England have deserved.

I feel so sorry for Wilf Slack, a quiet and kindly soul: in four first-class innings he has registered scores of 1, 15, 1 and 0. He is now close to the dole queue. Gower's scores have been 20, 17, 0 and 0. Gatting chased a wide one slanted across him. England certainly kept slip fielders on the *qui vive*. Richards has shown good judgement for best part of two hours – an innings which may enhance his Test claim. It is notable that Botham's 40, including three 6s, occupied him for more than *80* minutes.

November 11

Perth to Brisbane, via Sydney, and ample time to reflect what a very big country Australia is. About 2,000 miles, I suppose. About the same distance as London to Moscow? Anyway, with a change of aircraft thrown in, it takes eight hours, hotel door to hotel door. Everyone bemoans a piece of scheduling which has England playing (in sequence)

Western Australia in Perth, the first Test in Brisbane, then (after a game against New South Wales in Newcastle) the second Test back in Perth.

Four Western Australian players – Geoff Marsh, Bruce Reid, Chris Matthews and the wicketkeeper, Tim Zoehrer – are on the same flight to link up with their colleagues in the Australian Test squad. Reid at close quarters looks a genial beanpole suffering from undernourishment. But I must say that when he gets out there bowling it all comes smoothly together with an easy run-in and a model, high action for his type.

Atmosphere within the English camp as we await the second flight to Brisbane is not improved by sight of Australian tabloids reprinting excerpts from a John Thicknesse article, in the London *Standard*, terming Ian Botham a boor, a bully and much else besides. The complimentary bits, as I later learn from seeing the full article, are not of course included. What with I.B. v. Peter Roebuck, expected here shortly, and now I.B. v. Thicknesse, I conclude my daily filing to the *D. Tel.* with a reflection that it might be prudent for their reporter to find the safety of a neutral corner. I receive back a distinctly formal telexed message which runs: 'You must be neutral on Botham, Roebuck and Thicknesse but we must have any news on these confrontations. Sports Editor.' Not even a greeting of some sort, or even a 'please'. I wonder how E. W. Swanton in his prime would have reacted to this.

November 12

A hot, humid, overcast day beginning with the news that some while after this most ancient member of the scribes' union took to his bed, another much younger one, Martin Johnson of *The Independent*, got pissed enough in the bar for the hotel management, not believing him to be a resident, to threaten his ejection from the premises with the aid of an arm lock effected by the official chucker-outer. Apart from being a talented writer, Martin is a very genial member of the party, and I am glad to hear that his colleagues leapt to his defence, not the least of them Dominic Allan, a big, bearded charmer of a man who has just fetched up here to represent Independent Radio News back home.

Tony Lewis (*Sunday Telegraph*) has arrived with his sparkling better half, Joan, who has just enjoyed a month in India: a distinctly civilised addition to our strength, at once made evident by his immediate invitation that I should join them for dinner at the Sheraton where, thanks to an old Cambridge rugby contact, R. B. Collier (a director of the Sheraton chain out here), he is put up in enviable style. At the lush Gabba ground I also have first sight of John Woodcock, who is definitely our senior pro. This is his 30th tour. He says his back is mended. I enquire whether the tour may now officially start. Michael Peschardt, who has taken over BBC television news coverage from Mark Austin, has also checked in.

The Gabba pitch looks very green. No doubt its colour will change by the time the Test series begins in 48 hours, but Allan Border won't be complaining if the curator fails to shave it too close. The Australians clearly think their best chance of winning back the Ashes is to get off to a flying start on the two pitches, here and in Perth, where there should be pace enough to excite their fast bowlers. They have already announced a squad of 12 including only one spinner, the jaunty all-rounder, Greg Matthews. So it seems a simple case of which seam bowler they leave out. I doubt whether Geoff Lawson has been recalled without the idea that he should once more be their spearhead. I am sure Bruce Reid will play. Chris Matthews, only 11 first-class games, did well enough against us in Perth to think that he should now be due for his first Test. That would entail the omission of Merv Hughes, a husky Victorian who, with his drooping moustache, looks cast for a villainous role in Victorian melodrama.

England's management now comes under fire, quite

unreasonably, I think, for declaring today a rest day. In fact, all the batsmen plus the two 'keepers and the bowlers, Neil Foster, John Emburey and Phil Edmonds, opt for net practice at the Anglican Grammar School. Less happily, the local fast left arm, over-the-wicket bowlers asked for by Micky Stewart don't put in an appearance.

The English attitude is contrasted with that of their opponents, who practised either side of a media lunch given by the sponsors of the series, Benson and Hedges. Questions on the matter are aired at a rather niggly press conference attended by captain and management, at which the scribes seek 'unattributable' guidelines about the selection of a Test team not due to be announced until tomorrow. Management drop the wrist and play a very dead bat. The only newsworthy item to emerge is a statement from Peter Lush deploring John Thicknesse's assault on Botham. 'I object very strongly,' he says, 'to personal attacks made about players. In my judgement what was written about Ian was totally unnecessary, ill-timed and extremely hurtful. The whole side did not take at all kindly to it.' 'Thickers' is missing from the conference but admits to me afterwards that he had gone over the top. I meet a senior member of the team (whom I forbear to name) who says: 'Why should John get into trouble for writing the effing truth?'

I should explain that because of the time difference between the UK and Australia, reporters writing for morning papers will find their words overtaken by events. A Test match starting on Friday in Australia needs to be previewed in Thursday's newspaper in England. Thus the niggles at press conference here. Difficult to preview a match when you don't know what your own team will be, etc. etc. Heigh ho, we shall have to make up our own minds, rather than rely on someone else's – and presumably that's what some of us have been sent out here to do.

I re-nail my colours to the mast by suggesting again in The *D. Tel.* that Bill Athey should open the England innings with Chris Broad. I bemoan the fact that the side could have done with another State game, in order to get their act together, instead of the several one-day country affairs, worthy enough exercises but wholly irrelevant in serious cricketing terms. The happiest scenario for England, if the sticky, oppressive, cloudy weather persists, would be for Gatting to win the toss.

Pre-prandial champagne with Tony and Joan Lewis in their suite confirms theory that the Sheraton does them proud. He is to write daily pieces in the only nationally circulated newspaper here, *The Australian*. Good news. A very gifted writer. And it was good working regularly with him on television last summer, 1986, after he had taken over from dear old Jim Laker. No easy succession for him, as I am certain, with his sensitivity, he must have known. How wise that he sought simply to be his own man.

Another impersonal message from the desk 'ere I depart to bed. 'Inform sports desk of rest days in all Tests.' Can't he even say 'please'?

November 13

Eve of a new Test series. Gabba pitch *still* very green. Weather *still* made for swing. Ian Botham boomerangs it around in morning nets, one of which – thanks to inade-quate overnight covering – is wet on a length and too dangerous to use. England management register official disappointment while conceding that their opponents had earlier faced the same difficulties.

Peter Roebuck, hot foot on behalf of *The Sunday Times* (and well able to look after himself), arrives on ground. Will I.B. dot him one? Alas, nothing so dramatic. They keep their distance. P.R. is asked if he would care to comment on I.B.'s comments about him in Perth. 'I'm here to write for my paper,' he says. All good openers know how to play a negative shot. Carl Kershaw has arrived to cover the expedition for the *Sunday People*.

Anglo/Australian scribal gathering for announcement of

England team by Mike Gatting, with Peter Lush in atten-
dance. Athey to open with Broad. Two new Test caps: Jack
Richards as 'keeper and Phillip DeFreitas, only 20, as opening bowler. Only surprise – a welcome one – is that David
Gower has been asked to join selection committee: a move
long overdue which now gives him some sort of official
status. The captain says that in certain unfortunate circumstances Gower might be dropped down the order, Richards
or himself going in at No. 3. The skipper bats there for
Middlesex, and even though he has few runs behind him I
think he should be the man in such an eventuality. He confirms that if sticky weather continues, I.B. will be first in
queue for new ball, and the captain won't be arguing about
it.

Good luck to Richards, but Bruce French is unlucky,
having done a very sound job for England after taking over
from Paul Downton. So is James Whitaker with a hundred
to his name in just one first-class innings. There is simply
no place for him, for the moment at least, at 3, 4, 5 or 6 in the
Test side.

Much enjoyed din-din at Lennon's Hotel with John
Woodcock and Christopher Martin-Jenkins, who is pained
to hear me suggest that Gatting really ought not to conduct
a press conference chewing gum or even glancing at *The
Cricketer International* on his lap when ostensibly bored by
another damn-fool question. 'An excellent choice of litera-
ture,' the editor asserts – but takes my point. Our not over
articulate skipper is a good guy, well liked by everybody,
but he is still far too defensive on these occasions and still
offering too many bromides that fool nobody. All in con-
trast with his opposite number, who talks very well. I think
somebody should tell Mike that we (the Pommie lot
anyway) are all on his side.

I trust that all good Englishmen and true, 'ere taking to
their beds, are down on the prayer mat imploring whomso-
ever ordains these things that Gatting wins the toss tomorrow. It is a match, on recent evidence, which England must

enter sustained by the belief that cricket can be a funny old game and that the age of miracles is not yet over.

November 14 (first day, First Test)

A remarkable day, and at the end of it all we can scarcely believe that it has gone so well for England. Border wins the toss, his bowlers let him down and England make 198 for 2, Athey batting throughout for 76 not out to build a very handy platform for the morrow. England's skipper, looking like John Bull, gets 61 and Lamb is still there on 40.

I am delighted for Athey, who goes in today with a Test average of 15 (a top score of 55) and with a great deal to prove. He does just that. Technique and application exemplary, and scarcely a flaw as he bats for four and a half hours on either side of delays for drizzle or bad light. He looks what I have always thought him to be, a player of genuine Test quality.

Thank heavens England did not have to bat on this pitch yesterday. It still looks a bit green, but there is no great movement off it and the air is not so humid. Even so, Border must have felt like tearing his hair out as his bowlers (Reid an honourable exception) failed to find a consistent length and line. England come through an awkward first session for the loss of Broad, caught by the wicketkeeper from the thinnest of tickles. Gatting, rightly leading from the front, comes in next, survives some nasty moments and proceeds to play some robustly punitive shots.

It has to be said that Australia don't enjoy the best of luck this afternoon. When Gatting has departed, bowled by Hughes off his pad, Lamb lives pretty dangerously for a while. But Athey's head stays down, and, when he hooks, he is always across and outside the line of the ball.

In Brisbane, because of sudden nightfall, play finishes early, at 5.30 p.m. By then, on this occasion, the Gabba is awash. By then, too, we can reflect that England's decision to play their two spin bowlers might yet be rewarded. We wonder why Australia left out Lawson. Perhaps the Australian selectors know something about his recent form that we do not.

What a thrill it has been to watch, for the first time in my life, England playing a Test Match overseas. I like to think I arrived in good time at the press box but find all the best seats occupied by genial Australian colleagues knowing the form better than I do. The box simply is not large enough to accommodate everybody. Should I take a spare seat on the right-hand side from which I can see about half of the field, or one behind a window-stanchion involving a cricked neck when peering either side of it and, probably, the risk of lumbago in the shoulder as a result of the air-conditioning blast immediately behind me? Mr Engel of *The Guardian*, getting rather crotchety in a similar predicament, threatens to take himself off to watch the whole thing on television at the Mayfair Crest International.

Nice to see some familiar faces in the Channel 9 commentary box: Richie Benaud, Ian Chappell, Bill Lawry, Max Walker, Tony Greig and Bob Willis. Max is a bluff, most amiable character – indeed a bit of a card – who has, it appears, gone over big on Australian TV. Bob is doing the whole series for Channel 9. I wonder if they asked Ray Illingworth to come out. He was, I think, front runner for Micky Stewart's job but only on his own terms of work specification. Anyway, he likes to spend his winters playing golf in Spain.

I meet, for the first time, Bill Brown whom I watched when he toured England under the Don in 1948. A hearty thump on the shoulder comes my way from Peter Burge, a big, jovial man who made 160 against us at Headingley in 1964, and 181 at The Oval three years earlier. I have lunch in a private box with Greg Chappell and fellow directors of his insurance company, this second most prolific Australian run-maker in Test cricket having invited me to sing for my supper tomorrow evening with Queensland University cricket club.

November 15 (second day, First Test)

It's Saturday, normally time off for those who write for daily newspapers, but we are ten hours ahead of GMT and at lunch here (12.30) I am required to send six paras for the late London edition. Thank God you can be through on the 'phone in about 20 seconds flat. But not so good when a harassed copy taker at the other end puts you on 'hold' and you sit fuming for five minutes, wondering whether you have been cut off.

The longer I watch the play the more I regret the fact that I have no paper tomorrow (Sunday) in which to report it. I shall of course allude back to it in Monday's edition, having first covered the third (Sunday's) play here.

England 456, Australia 33 for 1 at the close, and Boon out of the way, after hitting a short ball from DeFreitas straight to Broad at midwicket. It still seems almost too good to be true.

We have seen a marvellous hundred by Botham, 138 with thirteen 4s and four 6s. His hundred, which occupies him for almost three and a quarter hours, illustrates yet again his determination to finish his last England tour on the highest possible note. But he works up momentum, when Hughes has the new ball, with an astonishing 6 over third man and two more boundaries in the same over. Later, he smashes that hapless but big-hearted bowler for 2, 2, 6, 4 and 4 in another over which has the spectators in a high old state of tis-was. By now – and it is only early afternoon on the *second* day of a Test match – Border has most of his fielders back on the fence. Talk about Bothamitis. The great man is permitted to advance towards his fourteenth Test hundred in singles. It is the biggest one made by an Englishman in a Test on the Gabba.

We have also seen a 50 by Gower remarkable for different reasons. It follows the swift downfall of Lamb and Athey, the last named departing to an excitingly athletic catch by Zoehrer, the Australian 'keeper, off an inside edge. Gower, first thing, survives a sharp but very catchable slip chance off Hughes. He looks in desperate form, but survives his luck until at length a pull shot ends in the hands of mid-wicket.

DeFreitas pleases Botham by the way he makes a very useful 40 on his Test debut – an innings all but cut off when he has scored a single. He edges a ball from Waugh down towards the slips. Catch or not a catch? It looks doubtful, but the umpire at the bowler's end, Mel Johnson, gives him out when standing in no position to adjudicate on such a close-run issue. However, Border suggests that the ball had not carried to him, and the square leg umpire, Tony Crafter (who has a much better view of the incident) confirms that it did not. So Johnson, egg on face, is obliged to reverse his decision.

I attend the University celebratory dinner and listen to a long, sometimes very amusing speech by a nonogenarian, Mr Justice Stanley, which ends with a standing ovation. When it is my turn, I tell stories, often retailed back home to mixed audiences, which get a lot of laughs, but sit down to what by comparison is a deafening silence. It was embarrassing enough to stand up in a lounge suit when 90 per cent of the males present wore black ties (my hosts knew of my predicament but Brisbane doesn't sport a Moss Bros). Oh dear.

November 16 (third day, First Test)

Third day of the Brisbane Test, and every prospect still pleases. Australia are bowled out for 248 and, following-on, stand at 2 for no wicket, 206 runs behind. Dilley has 5 for 68 off 25.4 overs – the first time he has taken that many in a Test innings and surely his finest performance to date. Now England's bowlers have a rest day for recharging of batteries. It can hardly be better timed.

The prospect is not so pleasing when Marsh and the nightwatchman, Zoehrer, begin the day by making 60 in the first hour. Both have their share of luck but it is too good to last. England work their way steadily through the middle order, Australia subsiding from 97 for 1 to 159 for 5. One of those is Border who goes down the pitch to Edmonds, to be caught in the covers, after looking ill at ease for more than an hour.

The fire and bounce of Dilley with the new ball makes further inroads, but Greg Matthews battles his way to an obstructive 56 not out. At one point I wonder whether Emburey should be recalled, but Gatting sticks by Botham, who comes up trumps with the wickets of Chris Matthews and Hughes. The English outcricket, save for a very occasional blemish, has been sharp and purposeful as the adrenalin flowed. Gatting gets his decisions right. Even the best skippers need a bit of luck.

After three quite remarkably good days for England I am wondering how the member of our union who reported to his paper that they could not bat, bowl or field, proposes to write his way out of that one. England can now congratulate themselves on picking both their spin bowlers, who may yet have the last laugh. Emburey has bowled all through the morning and beyond it, his control immaculate (26-8-52-0) on a surface providing some turn and bounce.

November 17 (rest day, First Test)

England's fast bowlers rest quietly in the city of Brisbane, others go off to the 'Sunshine Coast' which has so many ghastly high-rise structures that at certain times of the day they mask a very generous amount of sunshine from 'Surfers' Paradise'. Mike Gatting tells the scribes that he thinks the pitch might take yet more turn before the match is completed. 'In that case,' he adds, 'we should be in with a good shout.' He says he never had any doubt about the wisdom of enforcing the follow-on. When Australia are down, if not yet out for the count, keep them that way.

An Ashes battle between the respective press corps ends

sensationally with Australia beating England off the penultimate ball. Graham Otway (*Today*) gives several hundred
dollars to the bar lady for safe keeping, and is subsequently
distressed to find that she thought he was making a generous
gesture and had therefore disbursed it in free drinks all round.

November 18 (fourth day, First Test)

Alas for our hopes that the pitch would provide more turn
for the spinners. It does not; it gets slower, with less turn
and less bounce. So England graft hard and well, disposing
of five Australian wickets while their score moves on to 243
for 5, just 35 runs in front. Marsh is still there with 108,
having batted all day. By the time the stumps come out, he
has defied England's attack in all matches against them on
this tour for a grand total of 19 hours and 20 minutes. He
blends with his patience and well-ordered defence a variety
of strokes on the off side which compensate for a relative
shortage of them on the other. Not a man to give it away
tomorrow.

Things look good at one point today when England have
three men out, one of them Border, for 92. But they must
have been wondering where another wicket was going to
come from when Marsh and Ritchie embarked on a solid
century stand. The new ball provides a timely answer, Gatting availing himself of it when it is due and making two
perceptive switches in his attack. DeFreitas gets Ritchie lbw
with his first ball in a new spell. Dilley has that awkward
customer, Greg Matthews, caught and bowled off the leading edge. And it is a switch for Emburey, moving to the
Vulture Street end, which leads to the fall of Border, by
then looking dangerous once more. So, earlier, does Jones,
but Emburey has him advancing down the pitch and missing, Richards making a nice stumping. Border's wicket, en
passant, is Emburey's 99th in Test cricket. Ritchie, a handsome, aggressive player by instinct, settles for a responsible, quieter role.

At the day's end a gusting wind has the flags at the Gabba blowing in opposite directions, and rain threatens again. Thunderstorms seem close, but the forecast for tomorrow is not discouraging for English hopes.

November 19 (fifth day, First Test)

Awake, unusually early, at 5 a.m., to find telex from Sportsed. Eureka! Encouragement from home at last. 'Full marks Athey analysis,' it reads. 'Meanwhile, like light-hearted piece Aussie press teeth-gnashing etc.' So he enjoyed my piece on the rest day. I send him grateful thanks on my Tandy and, since it is still only 7 p.m. the previous evening back home, ask sports desk to add a para about Edmonds to my last night's report.

England's stunning victory, by seven wickets, surely has to be regarded as an historic one. What had there been in the run-up to it to suggest such a result? They have confounded prediction and gone one up in the series: the adrenalin is really flowing now. And of course it ends a long drought of defeats or drawn matches, eleven altogether, going back to The Oval in 1985.

It is Australia who have the problems, England who can hope to build from a promising platform as the two teams prepare for the second joust in Perth.

England may only have to decide whether they should pick two spinners once more, and perhaps reconsider the qualities of the two wicketkeepers. To have both Emburey and Edmonds in Brisbane was an inspired selection. Let us wait to see what the Perth pitch looks like. I suspect Australia will then include Lawson as their principal strike bowler. They should also consider choosing Macleay who, admittedly on brief evidence, looked in the State game in Perth to be a very good bowler of medium pace.

The last 5 Australian wickets are disposed of for a mere 20 runs. This after half an hour when there had been seemed little sign of a breakthrough. DeFreitas strikes a key blow by bowling Marsh off the inside edge. Emburey yorks Waugh for his 100th wicket and in the same over has Chris Matthews lbw. 3 wickets for 4 runs in 8 balls makes much better news. England have an end to bowl at now, and the innings is quickly polished off. Emburey's haul, which might well have been even more impressive, is 5 for 80 off 42.5 overs. DeFreitas has 3 for 52. What a first Test Match he has had.

When England go in again, there are some setbacks. For the second time in the match, Athey falls to a brilliant catch, this time by Waugh, who had earlier missed Broad in the slips. Gatting begins confidently but then gets caught at square leg. Lamb, failing to settle in, is given out lbw to Reid when the ball seems to have pitched outside the leg stump. But by this time Broad is happily established, and with Gower ensures that the celebrations begin at exactly 1.45.

Gatting suggests afterwards that he might have been happy to lose the toss: he was not certain that he had wanted to field first. As a skipper who has just managed to win his first Test Match, he takes things in a very low key. Not so Border, who seems to be fuming as he talks to the media. 'I know what it feels like to lose Test Matches,' he says, 'and another experience hurts just as much.' He is certain that he did the right thing in fielding first. 'Australia should have bowled England out for a lot less. I don't think we can play that badly again. But it will be a test of character coming back from here.' The fact is that in the post-war years Australia have never won a series against the old enemy after losing the first Test.

Botham wins the man of the match award, and no one is arguing about that.

By the time I have written day's report, put it on Tandy and fired it across the world, it has seemed a long day. I go to bed with sleeping pill at 10 p.m. Towards midnight, Sportsed calls from London. I am disappointed to hear that he thinks Brisbane is eight hours ahead of GMT when in fact it is ten. 'This addition about Edmonds,' he continues.

'Where do you want us to fit that in tonight?' I patiently explain that the addition had reached his desk in good time for his penultimate edition. It appears that his telex message omitted the vital word 'would'. He hasn't liked my thoughts on Aussie teeth-gnashing and now he would like something new. 'Can't have enough humour,' he says. 'Everyone's talking here about Martin Johnson.' I feel sure *The Independent*'s reporter is sending some colourful stuff but, bleary-eyed and semi-conscious with effects of sleeping pill, I suggest that if he really wants his own man to say that England can't bat, bowl or field, then perhaps he'd like to hire someone else, and have a second resignation on his hands in four months. He then gives further encouragement with the news that the front page, for which six daily paras were required on morning play in the Test, was printing about three of them.

November 20

John Woodcock tells me he also was woken up by his London desk last night. *The Times* called him at 1.30 a.m. 'Sorry to tell you,' a voice says, 'that your telex arrived all jumbled up.' 'Unless,' their correspondent replies, 'I was more pissed than I thought, it's my belief that I *telephoned* my piece.' Slight pause at other end. 'Ah,' voice says. 'I wondered why an Australian answered from your hotel switchboard. I wanted Dick Streeton in Karachi.'

I report my conversation with Sportsed to Chris Lander (*Sun*) who tells me of a singular triumph he had with his previous paper (*Daily Mirror*) when he was out here in 1984/85. 'Sorry to worry you,' a voice says down the telephone at 5 a.m. Australian time, 'but we're doing a round-the-world Valentine's Day feature and wonder if you can do something for us?' 'I'll think about it,' Chris replies, having just noticed *The Australian* newspaper being thrust under his bedroom door. On page one of *The Australian* there happens to be a splendid story about a man back

FIRST TEST

Brisbane, 14–19 November 1986

ENGLAND

	1st innings		*2nd innings*	
B. C. Broad	c Zoehrer b Reid	8	not out	35
C. W. J. Athey	c Zoehrer b C. Matthews	76	c Waugh b Hughes	1
M. W. Gatting*	b Hughes	61	c G Matthews b Hughes	12
A. J. Lamb	lbw b Hughes	40	lbw b Reid	9
D. I. Gower	c Ritchie b C. Matthews	51	not out	15
I. T. Botham	c Hughes b Waugh	138		
C. J. Richards†	b C. Matthews	0		
J. E. Emburey	c Waugh b Hughes	8		
P. A. J. DeFreitas	c C. Matthews b Waugh	40		
P. H. Edmonds	not out	9		
G. R. Dilley	c Boon b Waugh	0		
Extras	(b 3, lb 19, nb 3)	25	(b 2, nb 3)	5
TOTAL		456	(3 wkts)	77

Fall of wickets: 15, 116, 198, 198, 316, 324, 351, 443, 451.
Second innings: 6, 25, 40.

Bowling: Reid 31-4-86-1; Hughes 36-7-134-3; C. Matthews 35-10-95-3; Waugh 21-3-76-3; G. Matthews 11-2-43-0.
Second innings: C. Matthews 4-0-11-0; Hughes 5.3-0-28-2; Reid 6-1-20-1; G. Matthews 7-1-16-0.

AUSTRALIA

	1st innings		*2nd innings*	
G. R. Marsh	c Richards b Dilley	56	b DeFreitas	110
D. C. Boon	c Broad b DeFreitas	10	lbw b Botham	14
T. J. Zoehrer†	lbw b Dilley	38	not out	16
D. M. Jones	lbw b DeFreitas	8	st Richards b Emburey	18
A. R. Border*	c DeFreitas b Edmonds	7	c Lamb b Emburey	23
G. M. Ritchie	c Edmonds b Dilley	41	lbw b DeFreitas	45
G. R. J. Matthews	not out	56	c&b Dilley	13
S. R. Waugh	c Richards b Dilley	0	b Emburey	28
C. D. Matthews	c Gatting b Botham	11	lbw b Emburey	0
M. G. Hughes	b Botham	0	b DeFreitas	0
B. A. Reid	c Richards b Dilley	3	c Broad b Emburey	2
Extras	(b 2, lb 8, w, nb 6)	18	(b 5, lb 6, nb 2)	13
TOTAL		248		282

Fall of wickets: 27, 97, 114, 126, 159, 198, 204, 239, 239
Second innings: 24, 44, 92, 205, 224, 262, 266, 266, 275.

Bowling: DeFreitas 16-5-32-2; Dilley 25.4-7-68-5; Emburey 34-11-66-0; Edmonds 12-6-12-1; Botham 16-1-58-2; Gatting 1-0-2-0.
Second innings: Botham 12-0-34-1; Dilley 19-6-47-1; Emburey 42.5-14-80-5; DeFreitas 17-2-62-3; Edmonds 24-8-46-0; Gatting 2-0-2-0.

Toss: Australia.
Umpires: A. R. Crafter and M. W. Johnson.

home in Oxford who telephoned his wife, told her to pack her bag for a trip somewhere, then flew her out in Concorde to dance the night away on the QE2 in Sydney harbour. Chris shortly rings London back, ad libbing several compelling paras. '*Tre*mendous,' his desk says. 'Don't know how you do it. But have you got any pics?' 'Ah,' Chris says. 'I tried, but I couldn't get accreditation to board the ship.'

It appears that because Pope John Paul will be batting shortly in Sydney, the New South Wales match cannot be played where tradition demands. Mistaken local priorities? To Newcastle, then, in a Fokker Friendship twin-engine job landing en route at Coolangatta, hard by high-rise, concrete abortions overlooking the Gold Coast's superb beaches. Descent to Newcastle reveals inundated landscape: it looks like they won't play cricket for a week. We drive into town past steel mills spewing smoke across the broad mouth of the Hunter river, and the coals brought regularly to Newcastle from pits some miles inland. Entering our hotel on the promenade, we are all but blown on to the beach by a chilling gale that would do credit to Morecambe at this time of year. It feels just like home.

November 21 (first day v. New South Wales)

A spacious ground where the old MCC teams used to take on country opposition is miraculously ready for a full day's play in the most important contest it has staged. England, put in, total 197 after being 106 for 8. This seems back to where we were before the Test. But the pitch has moisture below its surface: conditions are none too easy. A good job the tail rustles up a few: Foster 25, Small 27, French 38 not out in two hours – an innings that should weigh in his favour when they debate who keeps wicket in the second Test.

Even Botham, 14 off 17 overs, makes little headway. Then he is given out caught at slip off Holland's leg break. He is not a man who hangs around when he knows he is out. He hangs around – to get what looks from the press box at square leg a poor decision. Another disappointment is to see Gower missing the boat again when he needs a long convincing innings. However, at the end of a day bitterly cold by local standards, the pitch is still turning and Emburey has nipped out both the New South Wales openers. Fifteen for 2 off 21 overs.

November 22 (second day v. New South Wales)

Today's *Sydney Morning Herald* makes a very good English read; the Australians are getting paranoid about that Test defeat as well as about their captaincy. 'The great captaincy debate: Should Border go?' screams the banner headline on a whole page devoted to the inquest. 'With so many things preying on his mind Border needs a temporary sojourn in dry dock,' writes the great 'Tiger' O'Reilly, who has never been short on firm opinion. 'The selectors should see that he gets it.'

'Allan Border,' asserts Ian Chappell, 'is the best man to captain Australia and there is no question about looking elsewhere.' I am sure he is right. Even Mike Gatting's views are canvassed. 'This is the time to support Border, not to shoot him down in flames,' he is quoted as saying. With a wry smile, too, I dare say.

It's Saturday, a day off for the dailies. But my word, the Sundays have a good story, if not of the ideal sort. England bowl out New South Wales for 181: a first innings lead of 16. Then they finish the day on a ghastly 66 for 9. So by the time the State side have finished them off by lunch time tomorrow, I may still have plenty of space in tomorrow's report to refer back to another chapter in the horror show.

November 23 (third day v. New South Wales)

We all know what follows the Lord Mayor's show and it is abundantly clear, as I have just told my readers, that England should stick to playing Test Matches on this tour and give the State encounters a miss. We lose by eight wickets, with about a day and a half to spare. Martin Johnson, who had written the 'can't bat, bowl or field' piece for *The Independent*, is contemplating starting another with the words, 'As I was saying when I was rudely interrupted.'

What caused the dreadful subsidence in our second innings? The time-honoured solution on such occasions: distinctly poor batting and exceptionally good bowling by Whitney (5 for 27) and Gilbert (3 for 23), two quick men who on this evidence should be in Australia's next side. Their excellent line and length puts their first Test counterparts to shame. Lawson did not even get a bowl on Saturday. Query Lawson for Perth Test.

England's progress around this vast country is positively bizarre, and now some nasty facts and figures can't be glossed over. Athey, since his splendid 76 in Brisbane Test, has made 1, 3 and 0. Gower, now pulling a short one, second ball, to mid-on gets 0 in his second innings here and we still yearn to see from him a long, disciplined innings.

This is the first big game in which Botham has played no significant part. It had to happen sooner or later, and better here than in Perth. Frustrated by the pitch, running out of partners and, for once on this tour, patience as well, he is bowled attempting to drive a good length ball.

It had been agreed by both teams in advance that, if the match should finish by 2.30, they would then play a limited overs contest for further entertainment of sabbatical customers. It ends at 2.41, England having been cordially booed for not appearing overkeen to hasten the over rate in closing stages. In fact, when it is 100 degrees in the sun, they get through all but 48 overs in under three hours, which seems quite reasonable. New South Wales, needing 99 to win, are 94 for two as the clock edges round to 2.30 and Edmonds has an over blocked out by Mark O'Neill, stocky son of the illustrious Norman. Great minds think alike. NSW have had to graft hard for their runs. The world's richest surfing festival, simultaneously unfolding off Newcastle's beaches, must have made for infinitely more spectacular fare. It hasn't been a pitch for stroke players but if 'Dutchy' Holland, who once made five successive noughts for Australia, can hold out for almost three hours, it can't be an invention of the devil.

Still time to see those surfers performing contorted miracles atop the enormous Pacific breakers. I reckon they could do it in a hammock standing up.

November 24

Only one change in Australian 12 for Second Test: Peter Sleep, the South Australian leg-spinner, for Mervyn Hughes of Victoria. Geoff Lawson, 12th man in Brisbane, remains a member of the squad. That surprises almost everybody but it simply delights Bill O'Reilly, who for years past has been fulminating in his newspaper about the need for Australia to field a balanced attack, whatever the pitch.

Peter Sleep is a genuine all-rounder. He made three Sheffield Shield hundreds last season, and another this, as well as 66 not out and 27 against us in Adelaide. 3 wickets for 382 runs in four Tests must do him less than justice. England think that Sleep will play to the exclusion of the New South Wales all-rounder, Steve Waugh. And all this on a Perth pitch on which, even though it has been recently re-laid, almost everyone supposed that Australia would want to launch a virtually all-seam assault.

It seems a heck of a long way from Newcastle to Perth, via that Sydney airport again, and indeed it is – especially so when you do it in an unbearably hot aircraft. Ansett have the gall to call an extremely ordinary main course for dinner 'Queen Victoria's Royal Treat'. For the third time running, when flying by Ansett, the supplies of wine evaporate when the drinks trolley is half way down the aisle in Economy class.

But John Thicknesse cheers me up with a nice tale about Sir Leonard Hutton who in 1958/59 accompanied Peter

May's side out here in his capacity as a reporter for the old *London Evening News*. Seated next door to the great man as they fly from Perth to Adelaide, Peter Richardson, one of England's opening batsman, is hoping to hang on his every word. The first one comes after an hour and threequarters. 'You've got to be very careful out here, you know,' he says in that confiding way of his. 'They're all descended from robbers.'

November 25

Performance of the week/month/tour? David Norrie (*News of the World*) became a father about a week ago. It transpires that unbeknown to mum he flew out of Sydney at about 8 p.m. two days ago, spent eight hours in UK getting to know latest arrival, and then took wing again to Perth, arriving here just over 48 hours later. 'Doing it that way,' he claims, 'you don't get jet lag.'

November 26

After nets at the WACA Mike Gatting kindly marks cards for the English dailies needing to preview the Test Match but not yet knowing England's side. However, it has been 15 months since their selectors, home or away, were able to indulge in the luxury of sticking by a winning Test XI, so we are not exactly writing in the dark. 'It would be nice,' the captain observes, 'to keep 'em one down in the series.' Even better, I would suppose, to get 'em two down with three to play. Anyway, I write for the paper that I hope I am not expected, in the light of England's dizzy, rollercoaster progress round this country, to predict the outcome of the second encounter.

Allan Border, who got so stroppy after Australia's defeat in Brisbane, has admitted that he may have gone overboard. 'It's history now,' he asserts. 'We've forgotten it.' He indicates that Lawson will definitely play this time.

'"Henry" is busting for a big performance.' He defends his field placings at Brisbane when Ian Botham ruled, but adds that his side mustn't get paranoid about the big feller. If Botham should rule again here, I don't think Border will adopt the Brisbane tactics.

'I shan't be unhappy,' the skipper says, 'if Sleep plays.' And that's no surprise, now that we have seen the pitch. Hard, dry and bleached by the sun. 'We could play on it now,' Border adds. Mike Gatting thinks it will turn. 'It could be a good thing to win the toss and bat first.' The Middlesex duo must be in harness again, that's for sure.

We are billeted this time at the Merlin hotel, an extraordinary edifice designed by an architect who can't have had to worry much about the cost per square foot. Its foyer seems as large as the forecourt on Euston station. Its interior spacious design puts one in mind, somehow, of Charles de Gaulle airport in Paris. But it is *very* comfortable: the rooms leave nothing to be desired.

November 28 (first day, Second Test)

Another remarkably successful day for England, in spite of everything that may have happened in Newcastle. No one can complain about an opening partnership between Broad and Athey of 223, so it may seem churlish to suggest that the final end-product, 272 for 2, could have been even better.

It is sad that Athey should have fallen for 96, so tantalisingly close to the hundred denied him in Brisbane. This time he is yorked by a floated inswinger from Reid, whereupon Lamb is caught by the wicket-keeper for 0 when framing a square cut. The captain makes an uncertain start, but finishes with 11 not out. Broad is undefeated with 146, and it is the sort of platform on which something very substantial should be built tomorrow. It is a peach of a pitch.

Broad has given no chance and has already almost doubled his previous highest score in Test cricket, 86 against Sri Lanka in 1984. His partnership with Athey is the highest for any England Test wicket on this WACA ground. They have been grateful, no doubt, for another wild opening spell from Chris Matthews, and for some bowling from Lawson which lacks its old hostility. Athey, on 3, survives a hot slip chance to Border off Matthews, but is soon playing some off side shots of quality. As lunch nears, he gets almost too confident, and I dare say Gatting may have urged him during the interval to proceed on a rather more sober note.

Broad on song is a splendid timer of the ball. He leans effortlessly into his strokes, which now have a wider range. It is splendid to see him prospering, for here is a batsman who bravely took all that was thrown at him when facing West Indies in 1984 and then missed out on England's tour of India the following winter because of a supposed weakness against spin bowling. Tim Robinson got the call instead, made some very big scores both in India and against Australia the following English summer, before enduring a torrid time, when he was in good company, in the Caribbean earlier this year.

I end my report for the *Telegraph* with a suggested vote of thanks to the curator for preparing so splendid a pitch, and with compliments to Gatting on his sagacity in winning the toss.

We have been hearing distressing news about John Arlott, who has been flown from his home in Alderney for a major operation in an Oxford hospital. But Jack Bannister, the former Warwickshire bowler recently arrived here to cover the series for his Birmingham papers, cheers us up with a little anecdote that John won't mind me recounting here. On a recent visit to Alderney, with John Woodcock, Jack was able to inspect the contents of J.A.'s cellar, which is considerably smaller than the one he used to keep in Hampshire. 'How many bottles have you got down there?' he enquires. 'Only 2,900,' John replies, 'but happily they're all for drinking and not for investment.'

November 29 (second day, Second Test)

We have had yet another shining day in the Test, but because it is Saturday my report of the play has to go into Monday's paper back home, a long time after it all happened, appearing indeed after the third day's proceedings have been relayed on the radio.

I mustn't grumble about that. England extend their innings to an impregnable 592 for 8 declared, and by the close Australia are 19 for 1, Boon having played on to Dilley. We have not just one hundred (Broad's) to celebrate, but three. Gower makes a resplendent 136 after beginning with hints of his hazardous progress in Brisbane. Richards strikes another (133) with increasing vigour and confidence. Some of Gower's strokes simply take the breath away. In such princely form he makes batting look the easiest occupation in the world. A glorious display is completed off 175 balls with nineteen 4s. Richards holes out when the declaration nears. To have a wicketkeeper batting like this, at No. 7, is a considerable plus.

Broad departs early today, for 162, unable to recapture yesterday's momentum. But to finish with such a huge score after Lamb and Botham have both made 0, and Gatting 14, is some achievement. It does not say much, perhaps, for Australia's bowlers, of whom Reid once again is the tidiest and most successful. Lawson has looked over the hill, but Australia give it all they have got in the field.

England's total today is the second highest they have made in a Test match anywhere in this country. Can't bat? What Border thinks about his bowling is another matter altogether.

November 30 (third day, Second Test)

The ball turned for Emburey late last evening, but it hasn't done much for him today, and in any case he has one of those days when he can't quite get things right. Play finishes with Australia 309 for 6, another 84 needed to save the follow-on, and Border is 81 not out. Perhaps the pitch will give something more when the match is resumed after tomorrow's day of rest.

It has been hard grafting for England, who at one time have four men out for 128. Only one, however, in the morning session: Marsh, who hooks a long hop from Botham to backward short leg where Broad, though tumbling backwards, holds on to an exciting catch. Jones plays some dashing, quick-footed strokes, though Botham looks convinced in a fiery spell that he has trapped him lbw when he has made a single. Waugh looks another exciting stroke player but he departs soon after lunch, caught at slip off Emburey. Jones follows him, taken via bat and pad off Emburey. But Border and Ritchie put on 70 for the fifth wicket, Border and Greg Matthews 81 for the next.

Border looks in prime order, Ritchie is a batsman of quality and Matthews is an obstructive little left-hander not easy to winkle out. Edmonds gets a much-needed breakthrough when a ball turns and lifts to Ritchie, who is caught at slip by Botham off the shoulder of the bat. Much later, half an hour before stumps, Dilley achieves another when Botham accepts a further chance off Matthews, who had made such handy use of the bat's edge against the new ball that Botham was employing two gullies as well as four slips. With so many runs in the bank, Gatting could still afford to attack.

Border leaves the field to a big ovation, having batted well-nigh impeccably for almost four hours, having struck thirteen 4s. He may not be the most elegant of left handers, but what a great little player he is. His defence is so well marshalled. He has an attacking stroke for every ball that can be plundered.

As an occasional ball is keeping low, there ought in theory at least to be some further inducement for the spinners. In that case Border is battling to save another lost cause. 'If we can wrap things up quickly when the game resumes,' Gatting observes, 'I don't think it will be the best pitch to bat on come the last day.'

December 1 (rest day, Second Test)

Time, some of us think, for a change of scene – to Fremantle, and the America's Cup saga, where thanks to Ian
Wooldridge of the *Daily Mail* we get the flavour of what is
going on. Wooldridge has just been hailed locally as the
most brilliant sports columnist in the world, a judgement I
would not dispute. He seems in special cahoots with the
South Australian challenge, and some dry bobs have a
distinctly wet and interesting passage in a chase boat out to
the tender servicing the pride of their fleet. Alas, it is not
doing too well and, at 5,000 dollars a day to keep the lovely
thing afloat, there are fears that the guys putting up the
money may soon decide to cut their losses. We later inspect
Alan Bond's yacht, a gleaming white leviathan which, I
gather, set him back by 28 million dollars or pounds, I am
not sure which. Channel 9 television out here are backing
Bond and Australia IV. Channel 7 have put their money on
Kookaburra. No interviews, I suspect, for the losers.

We also take a look at the media centre, which Ian
Wooldridge says is the best he has ever seen anywhere –
and he should know. Fremantle seems to have been trans-
formed. It might be in trouble if Australia fails to retain the
Cup for the next challenge three years hence. The one
scenario it doesn't want is a final not featuring the Ameri-
cans, and all the dollars their rich supporters bring in.
There is some concern that the bloody impoverished Kiwis
might get to the last round.

Back to base, to compose a piece for my readers tomorrow morning, by which time another day's play will be
reported on their radios and, shortly afterwards, in the
evening papers. So it has to be something 'timeless'. This is
one of the recurring problems for reporters covering a story
which is made to measure for radio and 'evenings' – and for
television, too, provided it thinks it worthwhile to pay the
earth for live coverage by satellite. But those writing for
morning newspapers certainly can't complain of being

under pressure. In four of the five Test Matches, play finishes ten or eleven hours ahead of GMT, and in the fifth, Perth, the time difference is eight. Perth apart, they are required to furnish brief reports of the morning's play for their late London editions (although John Woodcock tells me he wrote 600 words for this purpose at Brisbane).

I was required to do six paras of which, Sportsed subsequently and discouragingly told me, only about three got in. There's planning for you. However, when it comes to writing the full report of a day's play, time is certainly on the side of the dailies. I get it away, on the wretched computer when it works, by about 8 p.m. local Australian time which, even in Perth, is 12 noon back home. When the computer doesn't work, I feel like screaming for a quill pen or carrier pigeons, but fortunately there is a marvellously swift telephone service which enables us to get through to base in thirty seconds flat. You're then of course at the mercy of a copy-taker who might or might not know how to spell gulley, but most of them are pretty good.

None of the English scribes out here is working harder or more diligently than David Lloyd of the Press Association. He is unfailingly agreeable, polite and helpful in spite of a demanding schedule all seven days of the week. He starts with coverage of the first three hours of play for the last editions of the dailies, most of them provincial, back home. In perhaps nine 'takes' he furnishes 500 or 600 words with hourly 'leads' amounting to another 750, not to mention the score details every 20 minutes plus instantaneous note of every wicket's fall. At the end of a day's play he does a 'lead' for the evening papers of about 600 words, as well as more on 'quotes' from the antagonists, where relevant. He then does a story for the morning papers of another 600 words. All that is on match days. On others, he probably does 500 words for the evenings and the same for the dailies. I reckon he is earning his corn.

Christopher Martin-Jenkins is another such. He has provided his typical Test day schedule for BBC radio. It

Chris Broad, Man of the Test Series

2 Peter West studiously observes from the press box in Adelaide

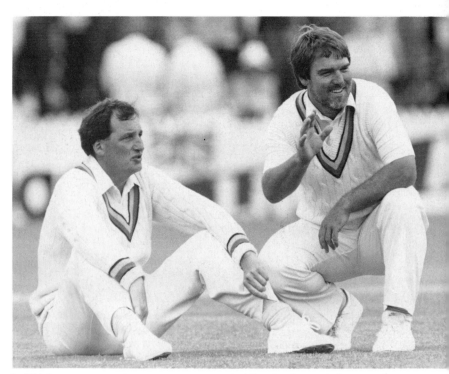

3 Middlesex partners for many years, captain Mike Gatting and vice-captain
John Emburey (left), now lead England in the Ashes series

Ian Botham flays the Australian attack in his brilliant 138 in the First Test

5 England's victory at Brisbane is one in the eye for Australian captain, Allan Border

6 Peter West and former England captain Tony Greig consult the Channel 9 Weatherwatch machine

Bruce Reid, Australia's leading strike bowler throughout the Ashes series

8 James Whitaker as a policeman and (9) Phillip DeFreitas as Diana Ross, dolled up
   for the traditional Christmas fancy dress party

10 A jubilant England celebrate the fall of a crucial wicket in the Fourth Test:
    Border caught Richards bowled Botham for 15

Gladstone Small, a late replacement for Graham Dilley in Melbourne — and Man of the Match

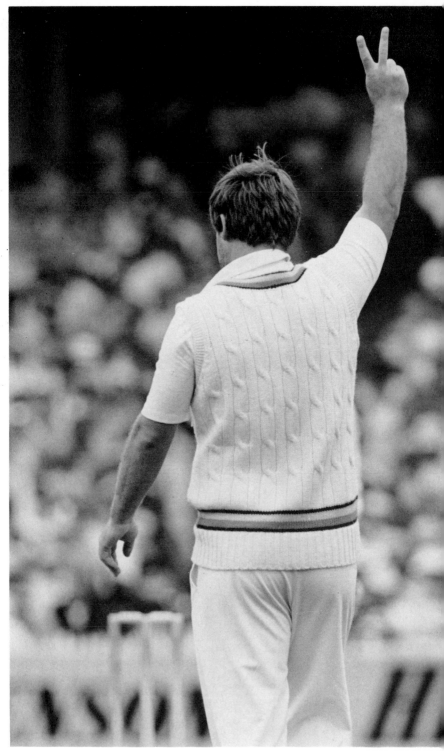

12 The England skipper, Mike Gatting, acknowledges the Ashes victory

demands 17 reports overall and six 20-minute periods of running commentary, one in every hour of play. All this demands a clear mind, the ability to write quickly and lucidly, and more often simply to ad lib. For someone whose hotel room is a shambles and who seems to be incapable of turning up on time for an appointment, the BBC's cricket correspondent is unfailingly on the ball, doing a very professional and wholly reliable job. The same goes for Dominic Allan of Independent Radio News.

The Merlin hotel is already bedecked with its Christmas decorations. Its bedrooms are beautifully appointed, the plumbing is of the highest quality, and the services provided can't be faulted. I can't stress often enough how unfailingly pleasant and helpful the staff seem to be in all good Australian hotels. They put most of our own lot to shame.

Peter Smith (*Daily Mail*), our wise and ever-cordial 'tour leader', has produced facsimiles of last Sunday's edition of the *People* which luridly asserts that 'King Viv' Richards, captain of West Indies, has regularly indulged in sex and drug orgies in Taunton. More intimate details about Ian Botham, who features prominently enough in the first story, are promised for next week. I feel especially sorry for Vanessa Tavare whose name – before she married Chris – is now dragged through the mire. Kathy Botham is now out here with Ian. I wonder what she thinks of it all. Ye gods, what a hideous muck-rake.

December 2 (fourth day, Second Test)

Australia save the follow-on, Border making his 20th Test century, and England finish the day on 199 for 8 in their second innings, losing wickets too regularly for them to make the headway Gatting wanted. They lead by 390.

The captain comes under sporadic fire for not declaring before close of play and setting his bowlers to work. Border says afterwards that he was pleasantly surprised by Gatting's decision. I am sure Australia would have thought only of saving the game, but there should still be time for England to bowl them out again. They must certainly declare first thing tomorrow morning.

Only two more wickets for England this morning, those of Zoehrer, who can bat very usefully, and Lawson. Border never looks like getting out. He has the answer to every ball until he chases a wide one from Dilley, and Richards accepts a low catch at the second attempt. Dilley has 4 for 79.

In their second innings England make an indifferent start. Athey is brilliantly caught by Border at slip, Broad is lbw, and Lamb very definitely so for another low score. That makes 3 down for 50, but we then enjoy a stand of 73 between the pugnacious England skipper and the silken Gower, whose batting had reminded me of a rake's progress in Brisbane and elsewhere but now looked sheer, easy perfection. However Waugh, medium paced, does a fine containing job for Australia. He has Gower caught behind, then helps confine Botham to 6 runs in half an hour before England's champion holes out to extra cover off Reid. The wickets keep falling as Border organises a good defensive operation while Lawson is off the field with a back spasm. Chris Matthews has been taken out of the firing line altogether after 2 overs cost 15 runs. Gatting gets to 70, gives Waugh the charge, and is bowled. A combative innings, nicely judged. DeFreitas and Richards each make a few before dying bravely. Reid, 3 for 58 off 21 overs, again impresses with his accurate line and bounce. Waugh finishes with 5 for 69 after bowling unchanged for almost three hours. He looks an extremely promising cricketer.

December 3 (fifth day, Second Test)

A frustrating day for England: match drawn – and Botham suffers a nasty injury. With no great difficulty Australia make 197 for 4 wickets before Gatting gives up the hunt with 10 overs left to bowl in the last hour. 'We only had a draw in mind,' Border says later, 'and we got away with one rather than being in the match with a real chance.'

The pitch offers England's bowlers far less help than its cracked appearance had suggested. On the rare occasions the ball hits one of the cracks, it does too much. And it is no help to England's cause when Botham, in sending down a bouncer, pulls up painfully, having, as is later revealed, torn a muscle in his rib cage. I don't like the sound of it. That could keep him out of action, as a bowler at least, for quite some time. We will know the full implications of it tomorrow.

After England's expected declaration first thing, they soon dispose of Boon again, this time when he is magnetised to a wide one from Dilley. Boon now has Test scores of 10, 14, 2 and 0. England are not the only side to have problems with their openers. No further joy for a long while. Marsh is put down by Botham off Dilley, in a fine opening burst, when he has made just 1 – but it is a very stiff chance. Marsh and Jones discreetly put on 126 for the second wicket and the game looks to be moving to an anti-climax when Jones runs himself out. It needs a fine throw from Broad at mid off to do the trick. Not long afterwards, Marsh departs as well. He is lbw to a ball from Emburey that actually bites, and he is trapped in front playing no stroke, having now batted against England, in Test and State games, for exactly 24 hours.

Just after tea, a ball from Edmonds, bowling over the wicket and into the rough outside a left hander's off stump, has Border well snapped up, bat and pad, by Lamb fielding at silly point. 152 for 4. Perhaps it won't be a draw after all. It might not be if Greg Matthews is given out for a bat/pad catch off a very confident Emburey, but the umpire takes a different view. Matthews and a restrained Ritchie then see out the remainder of the game. Chris Broad follows Ian Botham (at Brisbane) as man of the match.

Another letter from Sportsed, beginning with another

complaint from a reader. It contains a further reference to Martin Johnson ('I imagine he is popular with the brass at *The Independent*') and a cutting of a piece, amusing and waspish, that Frances Edmonds has written in her fortnightly sports diary for *The Times*. It related to her difficulties in gaining entry to the England celebrations after the Brisbane Test victory. 'A withered Oz-Cerberus defended the entrance with ferocity,' she wrote. '"You cannot come in here," he ordered. "You are a lady." There was no answer to that.'

'I would very much like,' Sportsed informs me, 'to have you using a wider canvas, i.e. items like this one would amuse our readers, much as I usually oppose "in" jokes. A diet of match descriptive needs to be leavened now and then.'

Sportsed has long been getting me down, so I compose the following letter:

I have received your latest letter and noted that as seems to be customary you begin it with a complaint from a reader – although on this occasion I am grateful to see that you have moved to my defence. It is a pity that your telex about Australian press reaction got garbled en route and thus misunderstood at this end. I had just previously filed what I thought had been a tolerably amusing piece on that and other lines, but perhaps it never got printed. I also filed from Adelaide a colour piece about the lovely Test match ground which, to judge from your most recent letter is the sort of thing you want, but I suspect it never saw the light of print. I'd be grateful to know one way or the other. If it didn't, I'll file it again, pre-third Test, and hope for better luck.

Do you happen to realise that I have now been in Australia for seven weeks, filing every bloody day and never a day off (I don't miss a ball on Saturdays either) and, apart from sending congratulations on what you term my Athey analysis, you have not yet been able to tell me that you have actually liked a single thing I have written. How does that seem by way of encouragement to a reporter many thousands of miles from home?

In the course of those seven weeks your desk has rejected the piece I wrote about Botham ending his England touring because, in its view, I did not project things forward enough and retained too many of his quotes. Yet what happens to my piece on the last day of the First Test Match when I declined to ventilate most of Gatting's vapid quotes? Two thirds of my report, under my name, is written by someone else, I know not whom, and all the vapid quotes are included – a day late. I thought it absolutely intolerable that anything of this kind could happen to a seasoned reporter without the slightest reference to him in all the many hours available before printing. I don't mind telling you that I came very close to throwing in my hand when some while later I found out what had happened. However, I slept on it, and next morning I came to the conclusion that I was still enjoying the tour in spite of an almost total lack of encouragement from the desk, and that you probably wouldn't want two resignations in the space of a few months.

Not long afterwards, no doubt as a filler at the end of my report on a day's play v. NSW, four agency paras were added including a positive *view* about Lawson's bowling. That again was something no self-respecting reporter can stomach, and I was subsequently pleased to hear that it would not be repeated.

You now tell me that you would like me to use a wider canvas and suggest that a diet of match descriptive needs to be leavened now and then. If you really think that my reports have been totally without a touch of humour along the line, I wonder if you have been reading all my copy.

You have previously sent me copy of an article by Martin Johnson, to whom you yet again refer in your last, and now you enclose a diary piece by Frances Edmonds with a very clear inference that I should write something of the same sort. I may need first to seek entry to a ladies' 'do' where males are excluded. But, more seriously, I am not Frances Edmonds and I am not Martin Johnson, both of them clearly very talented writers with their own special style. I happen to be Peter West, your appointment and your man, and I am giving it my best shot, believing that you hired me for what I am. I am trying hard to meet your needs in all respects, but I would ask you to remember that just an occasional touch of the carrot can mean a lot.

December 4

Another long flight, Perth to Melbourne, and Ansett predictably run out of wine, as well as gin and tonic, before we are halfway across the Great Australian Bight.

During the flight I ask John Thicknesse for his comments on my letter to Sportsed. He has no doubt that I am wholly justified in sending it. 'Group leader' Peter Smith, another old journalistic hand, takes exactly the same view. 'Good strong stuff,' says John Woodcock, an even older and more experienced hand. I sleep on it.

Much concern about Ian Botham and whether he will be fit for the Third Test. Inter-costal rib strains can be nasty and prolonged. Today it hurts him even to cough. 'I couldn't even pick up a bat,' he says. The team's physiotherapist, Lawrie Brown, gave him the good news last evening. 'It might be a week,' he said. Then the bad news. 'Or it might be six.' My layman's guess is that he *might* be fit to bat in the Adelaide Test, but not to bowl. I hope I am wrong on the last count. His absence, as one of our three seamers, would disrupt the balance of the whole side. But at least England have discovered Phillip DeFreitas, a quick bowler who should bat more and more usefully in the lower middle order.

Vibes from the Australian camp suggest that Geoff

SECOND TEST

Perth, 28 November to 3 December 1986

ENGLAND

	1st innings		*2nd innings*	
B. C. Broad	c Zoehrer b Reid	162	lbw b Waugh	16
C. W. J. Athey	b Reid	96	c Border b Reid	6
A. J. Lamb	c Zoehrer b Reid	0	lbw b Reid	2
M. W. Gatting*	c Waugh b C Matthews	14	b Waugh	70
D. I. Gower	c Waugh b G. Matthews	136	c Zoehrer b Waugh	48
I. T. Botham	c Border b Reid	0	c G. Matthews b Reid	6
C. J. Richards†	c Waugh b C. Matthews	133	c Lawson b Waugh	15
P. A. J. DeFreitas	lbw b C. Matthews	11	b Waugh	15
J. E. Emburey	not out	5	not out	4
P. H. Edmonds	did not bat			
G. R. Dilley	did not bat			
Extras	(b 4, lb 15, w 3, nb 13)	35	(b 4, lb 9, nb 4)	17
TOTAL	(8 wkts dec)	592	(8 wkts dec)	199

Fall of wickets: 223, 227, 275, 333, 339, 546, 585, 592.
Second innings: 8, 47, 50, 123, 140, 172, 190, 199.

Bowling: Lawson 41-8-126-0; C. Matthews 29.1-4-112-3; Reid 40-8-115-4; Waugh 24-4-90-0; G. Matthews 34-3-124-1; Border 2-0-6-0.
Second innings: Reid 21-3-58-3; Lawson 9-1-44-0; Waugh 21.3-4-69-5; C. Matthews 2-0-15-0.

AUSTRALIA

	1st innings		*2nd innings*	
G. R. Marsh	c Broad b Botham	15	lbw b Emburey	49
D. C. Boon	b Dilley	2	c Botham b Dilley	0
S. R. Waugh	c Botham b Emburey	71		
D. M. Jones	c Athey b Edmonds	27	run out	69
A. R. Border*	c Richards b Dilley	125	c Lamb b Edmonds	16
G. M. Ritchie	c Botham b Edmonds	33	not out	24
G. R. J. Matthews	c Botham b Dilley	45	not out	14
T. J. Zoehrer†	lbw b Dilley	29		
G. F. Lawson	b DeFreitas	13		
C. D. Matthews	c Broad b Emburey	10		
B. A. Reid	not out	2		
Extras	(b 9, lb 9, nb 11)	29	(b 9, lb 6, nb 10)	25
TOTAL		401	(4 wkts)	197

Fall of wickets: 4, 64, 114, 128, 198, 279, 334, 360, 385.
Second innings: 0, 126, 142, 152.

Bowling: Botham 22-4-72-1; Dilley 24.4-4-79-4; Emburey 43-9-110-2; DeFreitas 24-4-67-1; Edmonds 21-4-55-2.
Second innings: Dilley 15-1-53-1; Botham 72-4-13-0; DeFreitas 13.4-2-47-0; Emburey 28-11-41-1; Edmonds 27-13-25-1; Gatting 5-3-3-0; Lamb 1-1-0-0.

Toss: England.
Umpires: P. McConnell and R. French.

Lawson and Chris Matthews are due for the chop, and that Allan Border is keen to see Mervyn Hughes, who was dropped after the Brisbane Test, reinstated. England thought Hughes as sharp and accurate as anybody in Brisbane's early stages. Then he got savaged by Botham. He is not the first, and he won't be the last, to suffer such indignities. Opening the Victorian bowling two days hence, Mr Hughes now has a useful opportunity to push his claim.

With Botham out of action, DeFreitas nursing a slight ankle strain and Dilley complaining about a sore knee, England's side against Victoria more or less picks itself. We hear that Jack Richards will demonstrate his further versatility by bowling off breaks. Allan Lamb, who has gone off the boil, badly needs some runs again. Neil Foster, who hasn't been much in the action, should have a chance – if Botham misses the next Test – to get himself in lights.

We are now based at the Menzies at Rialto hotel, a rather splendid example of Victorian revival architecture, festooned with gargoyles and Gothic arches. In 1981 the site was redeveloped to include the construction of 1 million square feet of office space in two massive glass towers, and a luxurious international hotel. It has preserved the facades and features of the old buildings with happy effect.

December 5

Early telephone call from 'Wooders' at the Melbourne club, advising caution on the letter to Sportsed. 'Hold your fire until later in the tour,' he counsels. 'Then blaze away.' I sleep on it again.

Nothing has happened to allay fears that I.B. won't be able to bowl in the Adelaide Test next week. A specialist merely confirms what Lawrie Brown had diagnosed. I have a nasty suspicion that he might not bowl in the Fourth Test either. If hydrotherapy treatment gets him fit to bat and field, then he must still play. That, I guess, would entail another unchanged side, with the captain and Bill Athey dividing the labours of a third seamer. At Adelaide, John Emburey and Phil Edmonds seem cast to do much of the bowling, anyway.

England, one up and three to play, would be justified in thinking defensively, although to enter a Test with only four front-line bowlers involves a degree of risk. Bringing in Gladstone Small or Neil Foster – assuming Botham bats – would entail leaving out another batsman. Allan Lamb currently needs runs, so the more he makes against Victoria here in Melbourne the more timely they might seem to all concerned. But he is feeling very poorly tonight – 'struggling', as Micky Stewart observes, 'at both ends'. Small, Foster and James Whitaker, the last as the obvious stand-in batsman, must all be sniffing the air.

Yuletide celebrations start early for three of the players. It appears that Russell Harty has a television programme going out on Christmas Eve back home, so can Mike Peschardt on his behalf get the captain and one or two others to do a party piece for it? The Menzies hotel organises a suitable background by the swimming pool, with a tree and funny hats. Champagne is produced. At 10.30 in the morning Mike Gatting, David Gower and Chris Broad give a very passable imitation of being consumed by the festive spirit.

December 6 (first day v. Victoria)

First day of match against Victoria, and a minor English hiccough which will give the Sundays something to write about. Mike Gatting is not on the scene when the toss is due. David Gower deputises, and subsequently leads the team in the field when Victoria bat first. The media make enquiries, whereupon England's management, understandably seeking to protect the fair name of their captain, but not knowing where the hell he is, suggest that he is indisposed. Gatting makes a belated appearance, after which an inquisitorial reporter asks: 'How can he have been all that indisposed if he can take four good wickets?'

Finally, we get the truth. The captain had overslept. He had failed to hear an alarm call on his bedroom telephone, as well as some strident knocking on his door from Micky Stewart, who then had to assume his skipper had made independent arrangements to get to the ground. Well, it can happen to any of us. But except in one respect it is not the happiest week-end for the captain. The sports editor of the Melbourne *Sunday Press* comes out with a piece suggesting that at a pre-Test conference in Perth the press fraternity had been flabbergasted to see Gatting, in his England dressing room, beginning a conference wearing only a jock strap. Would not W. G. Grace have turned in his grave, etc. etc.? I wish, as one unflabbergasted reporter present, to put the record straight. We arrived early in the players' sanctum, and were lucky to be allowed in it, anyway. Gatting answered no questions until he was fully accoutred. What a sad abuse of journalistic privilege.

We bowl out Victoria for 101, and then make 128 for 5, on a poor pitch. The Melbourne square has been a problem for years. Many dollars have been invested in an attempt to restore pace and bounce. This one has bounce, but it is uneven, and there is deviation for the seamers. If we get another like it when the big contest begins on Boxing Day, the Fourth Test won't go the distance.

England must be grateful that Victoria choose to bat first, and that three of their batsmen, suffering from what is known locally as the Hilditch syndrome, hook Gatting long hops with unerring accuracy to Neil Foster at deep fine leg. Victoria's official scorer asks whether he should be using a rubber stamp. I dare say the captain would say he had bowled three vicious bouncers. Anyway, the pitch being sited on the far side of the square from the dressing rooms, the batsmen had ample time on their way back to observe their inadequacies replayed on the giant television screen.

Bill Athey gets out for 58 to the last ball of the day, having played, I think, as well as at any time this tour. He is without doubt the most severe and the most technically

64

correct of those in our side who like playing the hook shot.

Talking of the scorer, what a good idea it is to have the two officials – as happens on most Australian grounds – situated in the press box. At the fall of every wicket, at every notable milestone they disseminate invaluable information to those needing it most. And now I will ventilate another splendid Australian notion. Most of their sightscreens are made of gauze, through which spectators can see quite reasonably from the back of them. They are mostly constructed on rails, so it takes little time to adjust their position. Here is another area where Australia are some way ahead of us in sheer efficiency and commonsense.

I conclude that 'Wooders' has given me some sound and sensible advice on the Sportsed front. I file the original letter away, and compose a message to Sportsed, per Tandy, as follows:

Thank you for your latest letter. Can you please kindly arrange to have the second half of my daily allowance made available in Australian dollars at an Adelaide bank during the Third Test, and let me know which one?

I make mental note to spend it on his behalf, ensuring that his newspaper is represented in a style that E. W. Swanton would have approved of.

December 7 (second day v. Victoria)

Until it rains, and we lose two and a quarter hours of play, England enjoy a second good day. The last 5 wickets add another 135 runs, off only 29 overs, for a first innings lead of 162. This, in the light of recent experiences, may be an unpropitious augury for the Third Test. French (58), Lamb (46) and Foster (46 not out) all decide to live dangerously, which is the best thing to do on this pitch. The Essex all-rounder, as he would like to be known, finishes with a rather dizzy tour batting average (first-class) of 49.

Before it rains again, Victoria frustrate us with 56 unbeaten for the first wicket second time around. The umpires seem bent on re-starting even in a drizzle but Lamb takes the field under an umbrella, and they take his point.

I.B. shows barely marginal improvement and I am certain he can now be written off as a bowler in the Third Test. I am also very doubtful whether he will be able to bat and field. There have been, as promulgated, further lurid revelations back home in the *Sunday People* about some of his alleged extra-mural activities involving the distaff side. Peter Lush says I.B., though aware of likely publication, is greatly distressed and denies everything. 'As for myself,' the manager wisely adds, 'I propose to make no further comment on the matter.'

Made a boo-boo earlier today, having been invited to lunch by an official of the Melbourne Cricket Club. At the appropriate time I set off, following Messrs. Woodcock, Thicknesse, Lewis and Bannister, and joined a party which included the Australian Prime Minister, Mr Bob Hawke. I subsequently discover that I had gone to the wrong one. In such gate-crashing circumstances I thought it was pretty decent of Ray Steele, the genial president of the Victoria Cricket Association, to mention my name when he alluded to the guests.

December 8 (third day v. Victoria)

A surprise in the Australian team for Adelaide, announced here at crack of dawn today (and still with time to get it into the early edition back home). The Victorian skipper and left arm spinner, Ray Bright, is chosen. The inclusion of Mervyn Hughes, and the omission of Geoff Lawson and Chris Matthews, occasion no lifting of eyebrows. So Australia will have a choice of three spinners – Bright, Greg Matthews and Peter Sleep (who surely must bowl leg-spin on his own patch). Bruce Reid and Hughes must open their bowling. Steve Waugh, who had a good all-round match in Perth, will presumably be third seamer. Bright or Greg Matthews as 12th man now? In two Tests Matthews has taken one wicket, that of David Gower after he had made his superb 136 in Perth.

Gladstone Small takes four early wickets for 18 runs in 10 overs and Victoria subside to 112 for 4. I am very happy for 'Glad', an unfailingly cheerful soul and one of the nicest men in the party. It was a pleasure to have had dinner last night with both him and Wilf Slack, another very nice man, though more reserved.

By close of play, thanks to the Test all-rounder, O'Donnell, and to an obstructive left hander, Hibbert, Victoria finish with 296 for 6, a lead of 134. Hibbert puts me in mind of Bill Lawry, another cack-handed Victorian who gave England all sorts of trouble. Hibbert looks just about as difficult to prise out. The pitch is getting lower and slower.

Dinner, having got my daily offering safely away on Tandy, with 'Wooders', 'Thickers', C.M-J. and Jack Bannister, whose dry humour and ripe experiences as a wise old county pro make for excellent value . . . and so to bed. Alas and alack, not yet. David Lloyd of the P.A., God bless him, has been thoughtful enough to shove an official statement under my door. Back to the drawing board, with the following report duly filed:

The severe public reprimand that England's manager, Peter Lush, has given to his captain, Mike Gatting, for oversleeping and thus missing the start of the current match, against Victoria, reveals to what extent – as a result of pressure from the media – a mountain can be made out of the proverbial molehill.

The manager added that Gatting had acted completely out of character, had never been late for a game before, had apologised to the team and had deeply regretted what had occurred. He intended taking no further action.

Gatting may well have been the first England captain to have turned up late for a match. He is certainly, so far as I know, the first one to suffer this sort of public humiliation. Does he deserve it?

If we are to accept his own version of events – and he is a very honest, straightforward sort of man – then I do not think he does. There is no doubt that he put up a biggish gaffe. Of course he should have been on the ground on time. But he has asserted that after arriving back in his hotel at 12.30 a.m., very early in the morning of the first day of the match, he first telephoned his wife back home, then failed, as later realised, to place the receiver firmly back in its place. He thus also failed to hear Micky Stewart banging on his door when the rest of the team were due to depart for the ground. He simply overslept, which is something, as I suggested yesterday, that can happen to any of us, more especially if we have recently flown across a vast continent and are still suffering from time-change.

If in fact Mike Gatting, as has been alleged elsewhere, was not in his hotel bedroom, having spent the night with friends, then I can only suggest that he would have been wise to admit to something which any adult is free to do if so disposed. But Mike Gatting has resolutely denied any such assertion, and the manager has made no suggestion that he considers he has been misled. In such circumstances I would have thought private words, strongly phrased, would have sufficed.

If the matter had to be made public, then it would have been far better to administer it at mid-day on Saturday rather than to wait so long, and appear to be yielding to pressures.

Peter Lush said this evening that his captain had been severely criticised for what had happened. 'I do not intend,' he added, 'to rub the matter in further by imposing a financial penalty. If other incidents occur they will be dealt with on their individual merits. I do not accept that the incident has made it difficult for me to administer justice on an equitable basis.'

My reaction is simply this: that the captain made a regrettable boo-boo which has been blown up out of all proportion, that he has suffered a kick in the teeth from which I hope he is resilient enough to recover, and that he and his players may now be allowed to get on with the purpose of the exercise, i.e. to play some good cricket, hold on to the Ashes and not be diverted by trivial pursuits. [I subsequently discover, to my disgust, that the sports desk only reproduce the first paragraph of this report – more or less – and add to it three or four others which look to have come from agency messages.]

I wish I had remembered to say what had been my first reaction to the whole business: that Gatting should at once have announced that he was fining himself 250 dollars. That might have ended the whole sorry business there and then.

December 9 (fourth day v. Victoria)

What a relief to get back to the cricket, and a comfortable England victory by 5 wickets. Foster deservedly dismisses three of the last four Victorians and England, needing 184 at 4 an over, cruise in with 17 balls to spare.

Athey gets out early, cutting – not for the first time when playing a risky shot on pitches of uneven bounce. After that, it is a pleasure to report on the firm platform laid by Wilf Slack and James Whitaker, both cast so far in supporting roles. Slack's scores until today had been 1, 0, 15, 0, 16, 18 and 10, Whitaker's 108, 4, 6 and 0.

Slack plays serenely from the outset and is going thoroughly well when given out caught behind off what must have been the thinnest tickle. Whitaker could be forgiven a rather uneasy start but is soon punching the ball in front of the wicket. He relishes the hook, too, though not always playing it with certainty. He finally falls to a good one from Bright (called up in Australia's Test squad) who, thanks to Slack and then the effervescent Lamb, is hit for 54 in 10 overs.

If Botham is out of the Adelaide Test, the form of Slack and Whitaker is important. If the great man were to be replaced by a batsman, which I think is probable, then I suppose Whitaker would be the popular choice. But I suspect that the experience and greater steadiness of Slack might be quite useful.

December 10

The very likeable England skipper is not, I think, an unduly sensitive soul. An unabashed Gatting appears before the scribes who seek to write another meaningful Test preview without knowing what the England team will be, and marks their cards. Ian Botham can now be regarded as a non-starter, in any capacity. Better not to risk him, and have him raring to go for the last two Tests. Batsman or bowler in his place? Gatting says it is a three-cornered contest between Gladstone Small, Neil Foster and James Whitaker. I am sorry he did not add the name of Slack.

His verdict on the pitch is that it looks one of the flattest he has seen out here. *Ergo*, to go into the match with an extra batsman might still be seen as positive thinking if you've got the idea of making a very big score, and you've got two good spinners in your side. What if Australia win the toss, and make a very big score? 'In that case we'd have to do the same, batting second, and I think we can.' It sounds as if Whitaker is close to a Test debut. If they go for a bowler, I think it should be the more reliable Small. Foster can be more penetrative but also more unpredictable.

The captain is asked about his reaction to rumours that Greg Ritchie might be Australia's 12th man. 'Don't tell anybody,' he says, 'but I'd be delighted.'

December 11

I.B. receives one ball in the nets, which is more than enough. He is out of the Test, and it is later announced that James Whitaker will win his first Test cap and bat at 6. Good luck to the lad. He has been a splendid, level-headed team member, and he will give it all he has got.

My day is made by a visit to the home of the greatest run-maker the game of cricket has ever known, or is ever likely to know. Sir Donald Bradman has agreed, as Walter Hammond's most illustrious Australian opponent, to contribute to a documentary about the great Gloucestershire and England cricketer I am helping to make for HTV (Bristol). Sir George (Gubby) Allen, Bob Wyatt, Les Ames, Reggie Sinfield, Charlie Barnett and Sir Leonard Hutton are some of those whose recollections of Hammond have already been recorded.

I discover en passant how the Don failed at Worcester on his last tour of England in 1948. When I say failed, I use that word in a relative context. After all, he made 236 there in his first innings on English soil in 1930, then 206 in 1934, followed by 258 in 1938. The great man now tells me that when he played his last Test innings in Australia, against India at Melbourne in February 1948, he suffered much the same injury as Ian Botham has sustained and was marked down on the scorecard as 57 retired hurt. This injury was still troubling him when he got to Worcester in 1948, when he made a mere 107. He does not go so far as to say that he 'gave it away', only that 'it was not a very good innings.' If recollection serves aright, it was a case then of 'Bradman st Yarnold b Jackson'.

The Don is a splendidly fit and lively 78, now wearing a moustache. I happen to remark to him that three of his seniors – Allen (84), Wyatt (85) and Ames (81) – all remain in excellent fettle and that Ames, to my knowledge, still plays a minimum of 36 holes of golf a week. 'Tell him,' he replies with a gleam in his eye, 'that last year I managed 91 holes in three days.' He had won the semi-final of his B Grade club championship at the 19th, and lost the last round at the 36th. 'Don't write me off,' he said. 'I'm now back in the A Grade!'

Sir Donald Bradman is long chary of talking to the media, so I am very grateful to him for what he has done, to Gubby Allen for acting as go-between, and to Channel 9 (Adelaide) for providing a film crew.

Telephone enquiry from assistant Sportsed: could I tell him nature of Ian Botham injury because he wants to invite his London medical expert to write a piece? I explain, with as much patience as I can muster, that its details have already been covered in my previous reports. An intercostal one in the rib cage. I refrain from asking him if he has read my copy.

Then a telex comes in from Sportsed himself, advising where I may pick up my Australian dollars. 'Regards and keep it coming.' Well, well. I take that to be encouraging at last.

By local standards, it has been a filthy day for the time of year: windy, wet and distinctly cool. We hope for something a lot better tomorrow.

December 12 (first day, Third Test)

On this first day of the Third Test Australia, after winning the toss, make a modest 207 for 2 wickets off 92 overs, which is not the sort of positive progress one would have expected from a side coming from behind and needing to make the running. England with only four front line bowlers can be satisfied with that.

They confine Australia to 64 runs in the morning session, containing two brief interruptions for drizzle, and to 63 in the afternoon during which they pick up the wicket of Marsh. England's spinners, Edmonds in particular, are bowling with such accuracy that I am surprised to see Gatting resume after tea with Dilley and DeFreitas. Boon tucks into Dilley with three 4s in an over and is turning his attention to DeFreitas when the captain calls up his two spinners again.

Control is swiftly restored and, even better, Boon, having completed his first Test hundred against England, whacks Emburey straight to Whitaker, who clings on to a nice catch at deep mid on. There is an absorbing tussle between Edmonds and the dasher, Jones, quick-footed and eager to take the initiative. I can't remember seeing Edmonds bowl better. He restricts Jones to a mere 27 runs in a little under two and a half hours.

'Daffy', as DeFreitas is known, has his early problems on a morning cold and damp enough to remind him of Leicester on a nasty day in May: 9 no-balls and direction very poor. Dilley does better, but with little luck. On such a morning, we are missing Botham. But Gatting later contributes 7 useful, tidy overs, and DeFreitas bowls much straighter when given the Cathedral end, into the wind.

How will Australia build on their platform tomorrow? Jones is a clear danger, Border (19 not out) another. Ritchie can be a handsome aggressor. They will certainly need to get a move on, and I see no reason why England, if they bat properly, shouldn't go to the Fourth Test preserving their 1–0 lead.

December 13 (second day, Third Test)

Another goodish day. It takes Australia a long time, even though strongly placed, to step on the gas. After the expected declaration comes, at 514 for 5 wickets, Broad and Athey weather the last 8 overs of the day with much aplomb.

England must be grateful that with wickets in hand Australia decline to throw the bat until the last 20 minutes, when Waugh and Matthews hammer 49 off the last 4 overs. He really looks a good player, does Waugh. Prior to this late assault, Matthews had simply been pushing and prodding about.

DeFreitas has a further sticky spell, bowling down wind with the new ball, and Australia are away to a good start with Jones and Border making another 104 runs for the third wicket. Border eventually goes for 70, a score that England would have settled for when play began. En route he is missed off Dilley and Emburey, and finally departs caught by Richards when pushing forward to Edmonds.

Jones runs between wickets like a scalded cat and advances to a 93 full of exciting strokes when, shortly after lunch, he aims a hook at Dilley and is caught behind. DeFreitas, again more settled when operating into the breeze, has Ritchie caught at deep mid off, and England hold Australia to 89 in the afternoon off 29 overs.

It has been a well conducted defensive operation by the fielding captain, who plays his four-card trick and barely deals himself. Dilley has done a fine job when there has been nothing in the pitch for him: 18 overs throughout the day for 56 runs. England's spinners have gone for less than 4 an over.

I suppose I should not have been surprised to see some of my Australian press colleagues falling about in glee as England's bowlers were briefly hammered at the end of the innings. They certainly haven't had much to enthuse about so far. But by gad, sir, they do seem rather prejudiced. Perhaps those of us from the old country with stiff upper lips have learned to treat Kipling's twin imposters just the same.

Another thing that puzzles me is how many of my English colleagues leave the ground at tea time to tune in to Channel 9 television for the rest of the play.

The weather has changed for the better; Adelaide Oval wears a fairer face. Sitting in the sunshine, watching the seagulls keeping respectful distance from the middle on the lushest of outfields, I decide it is a very good place to be. Not, alas, during the lunch interval when we are regaled with an indifferent exhibition of American grid-iron football, and with a public address commentary on it which drives John Woodcock berserk as he strives to telephone copy through to London for the late edition of *The Times*. Bill O'Reilly asserts that not so long after he is kicking up the daisies, Australia will be totally dedicated to all things American, and God help the lovely game of cricket which, in his trenchant view, is long since on the slide, anyway.

December 14 (third day, Third Test)

There are moments today, with Broad and Gatting entrenched, when we contemplate a very large England score indeed. By the time it has advanced to 273 for 1, it looks a 600-plus job – and Australia under pressure in their second innings. Then Broad gets out, after making a second hundred in successive Tests. Then the captain, after making a pugnacious first one in this series. Then, alas, Lamb and Gower. So at stumps it is nothing like so rosey-hued. 349 for 5, and it's Australia scenting an opportunity to square the series. It's now a riveting contest.

How could all this happen on so flat a pitch? Because, as we all know, cricket is an unpredictable game and nothing, absolutely nothing, can ever be taken for granted.

Broad and Athey had made 223 for the first England wicket in Perth. On this occasion it is 112, Broad revealing a quiet confidence and a wider range of shots, Athey hooking Hughes and sweeping Sleep in the finest textbook fashion. Athey has made a polished 55 when he chops a ball from Sleep on to his stumps. It is too close for comfort. Athey knows it.

Gatting soon encourages Matthews to withdraw his close fielders from the firing line, clattering him for 14 in an over, but Hughes and Sleep do a good containment job for Border. Broad's hundred comes up off 232 balls: a 6 and eleven 4s. He looks well and truly 'in'. Gatting reaches three figures off just 140 balls. Every English prospect is pleasing. Marsh then spoils the vista by picking up, off a full-blooded pull from Broad, a stunning one-handed catch at mid on. We have had time to check that it has been the captain's seventh Test hundred, and his third against Australia, when he is indiscreet enough to pull a long hop from Sleep straight into the hands of midwicket. He almost always gives an impression that he thinks spin bowlers are meat and drink for his table, so we know just how he feels.

Gower survives an early chance to Boon in the slips off Waugh, but he and Lamb put on 58 with some ease, and we start thinking once more about a very tall score. Lamb, alas, then frames a very ambitious, back foot stroke at Hughes, to be caught at mid off, and Gower is lbw to a good one from Reid which he may have lost sight of. This is not at all the sort of situation that our Test debutant, Whitaker, can have envisaged several hours before. Emburey is the night-watchman. They get their heads down.

December 15 (fourth day, Third Test)

By the end of the fourth day in Adelaide, this Third Test Match looks to have taken another twist in direction. England are bowled out for 455, which is only 59 runs behind. Yet at close of play Australia in their second innings are 82 for 3, with Border 31 not out. The ball is turning, though not quickly, for Emburey and Edmonds, so it is Australia who are now under pressure. If England can dispose of Border early tomorrow, what are the chances then? I suppose that of all the possible results, a win for Australia is the least probable. I can't see them having enough time to bowl out England again and, since he is one-down, Border won't want to indulge in a fancy declaration.

So much for speculation. Now for today's events, and a morning in which, if things go well for England, they can put the match safely beyond Australia's reach. In fact they add 60 more by lunch and lose only the wicket of Whitaker, whose dismissal is a sad one. Having advanced confidently into double figures he has the luck to be put down by

Border at slip to Reid – a hot chance, certainly, but the sort that needs to be held. Whitaker, alas, is so disturbed by this incident that he tries an intemperate pull at the next ball and gives Matthews, on his birthday, a very acceptable present at mid off.

Emburey, surviving one or two dicey moments, including a stumping chance off Sleep and perhaps a bat/pad catch close in (since Australia are shouting for everything, one can't be sure), is soon indulging in his favoured sweep to good effect. As for Richards, the adrenalin is flowing after that hundred in Perth. He exudes confidence and good sense. But he falls soon after the lunch interval. 422 for 7. Time now for Emburey to indulge himself before he is caught behind off Reid for an invaluable 49 spread over all but two and three quarter hours. How well this wise, experienced old hand reacts to every situation.

There remains time for Edmonds to be given out caught off bat and pad, though he remains unconvinced. Reid has 4 for 64, and by some way is yet again Australia's best and most reliable bowler. Sleep finishes with 4 for 132. Australia have missed five chances, admittedly not all of them straightforward.

When Australia go in again, it's a comfort to see DeFreitas coming back strongly after earlier difficulties. His third confident shout for lbw against Boon simply can't be denied, so Tasmania's captain gets 0 after his first-innings hundred. Even better follows when Dilley, roaring in down the breeze, has Jones taken by Lamb on the leg side, off a perfect bouncer the batsman is unable to fend down. No further success, while Marsh and Border effectively man the ramparts, until Marsh, undone by Edmonds's flight, is caught and bowled.

It could still be interesting tomorrow, but England, as already noted, must be rid of Border without undue delay.

It is Monday today. But when you are touring, thousands of miles away from home, you sometimes forget which day of the week it is. I have been spied at the Oval by some members of the Kent Hoppers Cricket Club, not wearing the tie – as is mandatory on Mondays. This causes the delinquent an automatic fine of hop wine for all concerned, and quite right, too. I have always been very careful to wear the club tie on televised Monday cricket matches back home. Now at last I put up a bit of a black – to the delight of those here who found me out.

Alan Lee (*Mail on Sunday*) has flown home again, to take up a fresh challenge. Tony Lewis (*Sunday Telegraph*) departs this evening. I must add that the press corps is now fortified by the redoubtable presence of Robin Marlar (*Sunday Times*), who is here to report the last three Test Matches, as well as to take over from Lewis, in *The Australian*.

Peter May, chairman of England's selectors, has arrived with his wife, Virginia – I think just for this Test Match – but seems to be closeted with Australian alickadoos in the committee room, and we don't see anything of him. During his time as chairman, he has taken a fair bit of stick from the media, so perhaps he can't be blamed for keeping his distance. He has never quite trusted the press – probably for good reasons – but is now more flexible in his relationship than he used to be.

John Murray, erstwhile Middlesex and England wicketkeeper, is also here with his wife – and suffering from an early touch of the sun. I forgot to say earlier that dear old 'Ollie' Milburn was out with a tour party in Brisbane and Perth, but has now gone home, and that, although Peter Loader turned up in Perth, we saw nothing of that other Surrey and England emigrant, Tony Lock. 'Locky' did so much for Western Australian cricket, but seems now to have fallen out with the local hierarchy. He is said to be carrying a king-size chip on his shoulder as a result of the breach. That is sad.

'We must have news, news, news' was Sportsed's injunction early in the tour. Alas, I now find out, thanks to arrival of *D. Tel.* for December 9, how his desk reacted to what I thought was a big story: the public humiliation of

England's captain during the Victorian match. It rated three paras, and only one of those reflecting my own strong views was retained. Why do they want me out here if they do not print what I think on an issue of this sort? I remember that by the time I had filed a day's report, an up-date on Botham's fitness – with relevant thoughts on implications of his likely absence from Test – and done the Gatting piece it was 1.30 a.m. Australian time and it had seemed a longish day. This makes me wonder why I bothered to bust what I hope is a conscientious gut.

December 16 (fifth day, Third Test)

England, alas, don't get rid of Border at all. The ball doesn't turn for Emburey and Edmonds as much as I – and they – thought it might. Border (100 not out) and Ritchie (46 not out) bat safely through until Australia's captain makes a declaration on 201 for 3, whereupon England get 39 for the loss of Athey and Gatting before the game is finally interred as a draw.

So Australia are left to win in Melbourne and Sydney if they are to wrest back the Ashes. England are satisfied to get a draw after losing the toss on an excellent pitch for batting. They have contended more than adequately without the services of Botham, who is now making enough progress to encourage his captain to think that he will be able to bat in the Fourth Test. Some critics have found much of the proceedings a bore, and Gatting gets some stick for defensive tactics – which I think have been wholly justified. So long as the Ashes remain to be played for, captains will rightly see each game as part of a larger canvas. 'It was the best and flattest pitch we've played on yet,' Gatting says afterwards. 'We contained Australia and, if some people find that boring, so what?' – or words to that effect.

It had been up to Australia, after winning the toss, to take the initiative. A score of 207 for 2 on the first day – off 92 overs – was disappointing, but at least afforded a good base. On the second day they lifted the tempo far too late. Border admits as much now. He even says that he wished he had batted on to an even larger total in the first innings. 'Winning the last two Tests will be very tough but for the moment we've just got to think about winning in Melbourne, which might be a "result" pitch.' He hints that Australia are considering, for the Fourth Test, the omission of a batsman and the inclusion of another bowler. Just who, I wonder. Bowlers who can win Test matches are not too thick on local ground.

What is all this talk about Adelaide's blissful summer climate? It has been another unseasonable day: chilly, grey and damp. No early joy at all for England. Border survives a close call from Dilley for lbw, Ritchie what from English reaction is an even closer one for a bat/pad catch off Edmonds. In the first hour of the afternoon session Australia make just 25 runs while Dilley and DeFreitas send down 12.3 overs. I concede that it is not exhilarating stuff, but it suits the purposes of both sides. Border should have been stumped off Emburey on 85, and then proceeds to his seventh hundred against England, his 21st in Tests. The man of the match has hardly made an error.

Still time for Athey to be caught behind when aiming a pull shot at Hughes, and for Gatting, much to his disgust, I would think, to be bowled first ball by Matthews. No further alarms. 12 overs in the last hour are left to bowl when Border calls it a day.

I dine this evening with Phil and Frances Edmonds. Yes, he did have Ritchie caught off bat and pad, he says, and what's more, such are the injustices of life, he hadn't touched the one off which he had been given out the day before. I don't know why someone told me a little of Frances goes a long way. I find her very nice and very charming. We haven't seen much of her this match. She has got behind with her second tour diary, and has been knocking off another 10,000 sparkling words.

THIRD TEST

Adelaide, 12–16 December 1986

AUSTRALIA

	1st innings		2nd innings	
G. R. Marsh	b Edmonds	43	c&b Edmonds	41
D. C. Boon	c Whitaker b Emburey	103	lbw b DeFreitas	0
D. M. Jones	c Richards b Dilley	93	c Lamb b Dilley	2
A. R. Border*	c Richards b Edmonds	70	not out	100
G. M. Ritchie	c Broad b DeFreitas	36	not out	46
G. R. J. Matthews	not out	73		
S. R. Waugh	not out	79		
Extras	(lb 2, nb 15)	17	(b 4, lb 6, nb 2)	12
TOTAL	(5 wkts dec)	514	(3 wkts dec)	201

Did not bat: P. R. Sleep, G. C. Dyer†, M. G. Hughes, B. A. Reid.

Fall of wickets: 113, 185, 311, 333, 368.
Second innings: 1, 8, 77.

Bowling: Dilley 32-3-111-1; DeFreitas 32-4-128-1; Emburey 46-11-117-1; Edmonds 52-14-134-2; Gatting 9-1-22-0.
Second innings: Dilley 21-8-38-1; DeFreitas 16-5-36-1; Emburey 22-6-50-0; Edmonds 29-7-63-1; Gatting 2-1-4-0.

ENGLAND

	1st innings		2nd innings	
B. C. Broad	c Marsh b Waugh	116	not out	15
C. W. J. Athey	b Sleep	55	c Dyer b Hughes	12
M. W. Gatting*	c Waugh b Sleep	100	b Matthews	0
A. J. Lamb	c Matthews b Hughes	14	not out	9
D. I. Gower	lbw b Reid	38		
J. E. Emburey	c Dyer b Reid	49		
J. J. Whitaker	c Matthews b Reid	11		
C. J. Richards†	c Jones b Sleep	29		
P. A. J. DeFreitas	not out	4		
P. H. Edmonds	c Border b Sleep	13		
G. R. Dilley	b Reid	0		
Extras	(b 4, lb 14, w 4, nb 4)	26	(b 2, lb 1)	3
TOTAL		455	(2 wkts)	39

Fall of wickets: 112, 273, 283, 341, 341, 361, 422, 439, 454.
Second innings: 21, 22.

Bowling: Hughes 30-8-82-1; Reid 28.4-8-64-4; Sleep 47-14-132-4; Matthews 23-1-102-0; Border 1-0-1-0; Waugh 19-4-56-1.
Second innings: Hughes 7-2-16-1; Waugh 3-1-10-0; Matthews 8-4-10-1; Sleep 5-5-0-0.

Toss: Australia.
Umpires: A. R. Crafter and S. G. Randell.

December 17

Adelaide to Hobart, via Melbourne, the umpteenth airborne hop following five hard days of Test cricket without remission. Four days against Tasmania starting tomorrow. It's a tough schedule for the players – unreasonably so. As soon as this one is over, it's off to Canberra for a one-dayer against the Prime Minister's XI, so there's not much time to enjoy this lovely island. Not that we could see much of it as we came in, the hills surrounding Hobart being enshrouded by rain clouds. We are billeted at the Wrest Point Federal, which has a casino, the first of its kind in Australia. The view over the Hobart waterfront is beautiful, even on a dirty afternoon.

Encouraging news about Ian Botham, who has recovered quickly enough to be thinking of getting into the nets here. Assuming he plays as a batsman in the Fourth Test, England will have the same selection problem. I think they will play it the same way. Gatting could be a very adequate third seamer on the Melbourne pitch. I dare say there will be debate about whether DeFreitas gets the new ball again with Dilley. He had a mixed match at Adelaide, bowling two poor spells down wind. This might have rocked the confidence of an intensely committed and ambitious young cricketer, but he was sympathetically handled by his captain and, to his credit, recovered poise, length and direction when bowling at the other end. His batting, already useful, should get better. He is an outstandingly lissom and mobile outfielder.

December 18 (first day v. Tasmania)

No play today, unsurprisingly. We could scarcely distinguish the pitch from the square, it was so lush and unprepared. Last year, Tasmania v. India, not a ball was bowled in four days. But the setting is as spectacular, surely, as in any major cricketing centre in the world.

Bruce French has been one of the unlucky players on this

tour. Having lost his Test place to Jack Richards, though always remaining cheerful and a thoroughly good team man, he has been suffering chest pains for a day or so, has had a cardiac check (with happy results), but has now entered a local hospital on doctor's advice for further examination. To think that although he kept wicket so well for England back home last summer, he has yet – on three tours – to do so for them in a Test Match overseas.

Richard Ellison of Kent is playing for Tasmania, so an interview with him seems appropriate. Against Australia in the last two Cornhill Tests of 1985 he took 17 wickets at the remarkable average of 10.88. Last summer back home he suffered such a loss of form and confidence that he finished the season with only 22 championship wickets altogether. Now it seems he has discovered the old rhythm again. He is a popular, respected figure here. They like his unstinting effort.

December 19 (second day v. Tasmania)

The astonishing news is that I.B. has batted and *bowled* in an indoor net, and is none the worse for it. Reaction awaited. If all goes well, he will have a more thorough work-out two days hence and then play in the one-day game in Canberra. It is of course the most cheering news we could have. Clearly we should never have underestimated the recovery powers of an immensely strong and resilient character.

Bruce French has had some inconclusive hospital tests and is back on board, it is thought with one of these mysterious viruses.

At the cricket, Mike Gatting wins a good toss and England bowl out Tasmania for 79, Richard Ellison obstructing them for an hour and a half. Movement for the seamers and, more importantly, steepish bounce, especially at one end, where Neil Foster has 4 for 20. Phillip DeFreitas also gets 4, and Gladstone Small, bowling 13 successive overs into half a gale, obtains 2 for just 8. All the catches stick. In the sunny but still cool and blustery evening, England make 73 for the loss of Chris Broad. Slack, 37 not out, looks as composed as he had done against Victoria.

December 20 (third day v. Tasmania)

Off at crack of dawn to watch Ian Botham, Phil Edmonds and John Woodcock fish for trout in the centre of this lovely island. Ian has suffered no significant reaction from his net and is more than pleased to have won himself 7,000 dollars (over £3,000) in the hotel casino last evening.

London Lakes are the creation of a Tasmanian, Jason Garrett, who bought himself 4,500 acres over a decade ago, made two areas of water with a river between them, and built a sumptuous log-cabin retreat for those who seek comfort and perfect serenity in idyllic surroundings. Fishing, of course, is the great 'therapy' of Ian Botham's life. I don't doubt he will return to London Lakes when he plays for Queensland.

'Wooders', who was born with his feet in the River Test and has been catching trout on a dry fly ever since, gets off the mark with the fish of the day, a lovely brown trout of 5 lbs. After that, though, I.B., more familiar with the wet fly method better suited to the conditions, takes the lead. Final score: *The Times* 1, the *Sun* 3.

Philippe Edmonds, who was casting a fly for the first time, also catches one, but Brian Davison (Rhodesia, Leicestershire, Gloucestershire and Tasmania), who was kind enough to invite me along, fails to trouble the scorers. Brian, now nudging 40, was one of the hardest hitters of a cricket ball I have seen. He has retired from the game, joining a reform group which has ousted the board of management of the Tasmanian Cricket Association in Hobart. He is now an executive on the TCA as well as the Tasmanian Cricket Council, which administers cricket throughout the island. I think he will make things hum.

England declare with a first innings lead of 262 and then get 3 Tasmanian wickets for 43. So an early finish is anticipated tomorrow. The star of the batting show is John Emburey who strikes ten 4s and one 6 in an innings of 46. Wilf Slack gets 89, by a long way his highest of the tour, Athey compiles a boring 30 not out, and Richard Ellison, waiting for a steepling catch to swirl down in a howling gale, misses contact by several yards. Neil Foster with 25 keeps his average in the 40s.

December 21 (fourth day v. Tasmania)

No undue trouble for quick bowlers on a pitch colourfully described by Tasmania's captain, David Boon, as 'a crook deck'. England bowl them out for 167 to win by an innings and 96 runs. A hard day for all concerned: the wind blows even more strongly, its origins surely in Antarctica. But it has been a businesslike job by England all round.

There is some concern about yet another modest score (19) by Lamb, who has not passed 50 in his last eight innings, but Micky Stewart observes afterwards that there would be more worry if he were not hitting the ball in the middle of the bat. I'm reminded of the – I think – Greg Chappell quote following a sequence of low scores: 'It's not that I'm playing badly. It's just that I keep getting out.'

Stewart also tells the media that the form of Gladstone Small and Neil Foster was such as to cause no worries should either of them be chosen for the Fourth Test. Someone asks whether Phillip DeFreitas has gone off the boil. I was glad to hear Stewart's reply:'He's doing fine. No one can expect total consistency from a 20-year-old.'

The latest news about Ian Botham is somewhat more guarded. He has suffered a bit of reaction following his net two days ago. This is understandable. England can't yet count on him as a bowler in the Melbourne Test. But the good news about I.B. is that he came through a random breathalyser test with flying colours when driving home from his fishing trip last night. Such had been his abstinence that he registered a score of zero, which I think would not have been the case had the test been applied to 'Wooders', who was occupying the seat next to the driver.

December 22

Onwards, via Melbourne again, to Canberra. None of us, I dare say, is sorry to be saying goodbye to those Tasmanian winds, but I would like to have seen more of the island in happier weather.

The team, as well as nine wives now with them, and a few scribes (of which I fortunately am one) are invited to the Prime Minister's cocktail reception in the garden of his official residence, The Lodge. Some of the scribes who don't get a touch are understandably aggrieved. A case, I think, of all or none getting invited, but I keep a low profile on the issue and meekly accept a late invitation through tour leader Peter Smith.

I am glad I do, because Arthur Morris, Neil Harvey and Alan Davidson are among the guests, and it is a joy to talk again to old friends and heroes from yesteryear. What with the presence at the party of Allan Border and David Gower, it is quite a muster of illustrious left-handed batsmen. I might add that none of the old Australian trio has much to say for the present quality of their Test bowling.

The gathering is also notable for the presence of 'Stork' Hendry, at 91 the oldest surviving Anglo/Australian Test cricketer, who first played against England, would you believe it, in 1921. He was Australia's oldest representative at the Cornhill Centenary Test at Lord's in 1980. I treasure the memory of a television chat I had with him and Percy Fender, now no longer with us. 'Stork' remains in sparkling form.

One of the PM's aides tells me that when the morning papers are put before him so that he can test the daily political pulse of the nation, he first turns to the back pages to get himself up to date with the cricket news. This seems to me to show a very proper sense of priorities. Mr Hawke, of course, was a good player in his day, and I think an Authentic at Oxford. He has done the game in these parts a good turn by reviving, four seasons ago, a fixture against the touring side that was traditional in the days of Sir Robert Menzies.

A posse of television crews, with cameras, buzz round the gathering all evening and, needless to say, they all want a picture of PM and you-know-who. I can't quite see this sort of thing happening in the garden at No. 10 Downing Street.

Australia have named their 12 for the Melbourne Test: Craig McDermott, the Queensland fast bowler, has been recalled, and Ray Bright, the Victorian captain and left arm spinner, has been dumped after being 12th man in Adelaide. There can be no doubt that Australia intend to go into the match with four seam bowlers – McDermott, Reid, Hughes and Waugh.

December 23 (one-day match v. Prime Minister's XI)

We have not seen too much of Australian sunshine during the last three weeks in Melbourne, Adelaide and Hobart. But my word, we find it again in the capital city of Canberra. The game is played on the tree-fringed Manuka Oval in front of a full house of 8,000 spectators enjoying themselves under a cloudless sky.

It is the day when I.B. plays his first game since early in December. He bowls his stint of ten overs, off a short run, at medium pace but still sharp enough to have Jack Richards standing back, and he takes 2 wickets for 42. Later, after a prudent start to his innings, he plunders the bowling to the tune of 43 off 44 balls until he is caught at long off when seeking to carry the boundary. He says afterwards that he suffered no reaction except one slight twinge when leaping high to his left hand side in the field. 'I won't be able to bowl flat out for perhaps another fortnight, but I'll be at 75 per cent for the Test and I'm very happy about my batting. I think I can do an adequate job as third seamer.'

I agree with that, but Jack Bannister, a wise old Warwickshire pro., is one that does not. Botham now seems certain to play in the Test, but the doubts about his capacity as a bowler may strengthen England's inclination to include a fourth seam bowler. I expect now that they will pick 12: the side that played in the Adelaide Test, except that Botham will be back instead of James Whitaker, plus Gladstone Small or Neil Foster. Small would be the safer bet, with his greater accuracy and consistency, Foster the more adventurous one. But England are one up and two to play; they are not in business to gamble. There will come a time in the Test when they will need to defend on a very spacious arena. I hope John Emburey and Phil Edmonds are retained in a balanced attack. I hope it is not wishful thinking to believe that Graham Dilley, Phillip DeFreitas, Ian Botham and Mike Gatting can look after the seam department on what is thought to be a 'result' pitch.

Its character has caused much concern for the best part of a decade. Now, in an effort to restore a better, more even bounce, half of the square has been relaid. The Fourth Test will be played on the old half, where the curator has had a battery of arc lamps to encourage new growth. If it is to last the course, there will be some moisture in it first thing. Neil Harvey has no doubt whatsoever that the captain winning the toss must give his quick bowlers first crack of the whip. Fingers crossed for Mike Gatting when Allan Border spins the coin. Whatever happens, England are enviably placed. Border has said that it would be asking a lot, even of West Indies, to win the last two Tests. But nothing less will do for Australia if those Ashes are to be regained.

Back to Melbourne in the evening, and I must not forget to add that England beat the Prime Minister's XI by 4 wickets, Broad making a fluent 47, Gatting a punitive 30 and Gower doing much as he pleased for 68.

Australia have named a 14-man squad for the quadrangular Benson and Hedges one-day Challenge matches, due in Perth in the first week of 1987, and have left out three of their Test players, Greg Ritchie, Peter Sleep and Mervyn Hughes. Ritchie's fielding must count against him in the pyjama game. No weight of support for Sleep's leg spin in such a contest. The omission of Hughes is more surprising, due, no doubt, to an Australian desire to have bowlers who can bat. This certainly would apply to the call-up of Simon O'Donnell (Victoria) and Ken Macleay (Western Australia). Mike Whitney (New South Wales) is another addition; he must have been very close to Test selection. We don't know a lot about Simon Davis, the Victorian quick bowler, but he has been on the one-day scene for some time. Glenn Bishop (South Australia) looked an upstanding, handsome and aggressive batsman when we met him in the State game in Adelaide, and he played another good innings against us in Canberra.

December 24

I have found it hard, in an Australian summer, to catch the festive Christmas spirit but at lunch today, with Phil and Frances Edmonds, a choir of boys and girls sings 'Silent Night' in the Menzies at Rialto restaurant. Of a sudden home seems so far away, and I can scarcely hold back my tears.

Now we know that England have chosen a squad of 13: Botham for Whitaker, Gladstone Small and Neil Foster added. All eventualities covered for a pitch which, at this distance, has got the pundits puzzled. They think it might seam at one end, turn at the other. More will be revealed on Boxing Day morning.

Telex from Sportsed, who must have been impressed by the lighthearted piece I wrote about the greatest of run-getters: 'Please file major feature on Bradman – his views on modern cricket, England, Australia, Botham, etc.' Well, he said 'Please', which is nice. I reply as tactfully as I can on Tandy that my visit to Sir Donald's home in Adelaide, finessed for me by Sir George (Gubby) Allen, had been a one-off to obtain a tribute from Walter Hammond's greatest Australian opponent for a documentary on HTV Bristol. The piece I subsequently wrote for the paper had to be an unexpected bonus. Sir Donald has long been distrustful of the media. Reporters have been busting their gut for years to get him to talk about times past and times present. I didn't think he would agree to talk to me on the topics suggested, but I thought I might have his confidence, and I would do my best.

So I write to Sir Donald, pleading Sportsed's case, and ask him whether he would agree to be interviewed when I am next in Adelaide, in the New Year, or to answer questions through the post. I enclose a stamped envelope addressed to me in Perth, our next port of call. I think I already know what his reply will be.

December 25

It is traditional that the media fork out for a party on Christmas morning attended by all the team and their wives. A happy, relaxed occasion is brought to a very amusing climax when some of the scribes, inspired by scriptwriter David Norrie, mount a sketch based on the England captain's lie-in during the Victorian game. It gets a lot of laughs, not least from the skipper. After this, the players depart for a traditional lunch in fancy dress, and it is attended for the first time by their wives, which seems a civilised addition long overdue. The media move off for a prolonged and very bibulous lunch at a local restaurant during which David Norrie again demonstrates his flair for showbiz by conducting a *This is Your Life* on our doyen, John Woodcock, which goes down a treat. Highlights of this show are recorded messages from E. W. Swanton, John Arlott, Richie Benaud and Tony Greig, all splendidly impersonated by Christopher Martin-Jenkins, who has a rare talent for such things.

For the record, the players' cast list at the fancy dress party is as follows: Mike Gatting, *D'Artagnan*; John Emburey, *Monk*; Bill Athey, *Master of Arts*; Ian Botham, *Bunny Buntham*; Chris Broad, *King of Siam*; Phillip DeFreitas, *Diana Ross*; Graham Dilley, *David Gower* (dripping champagne); Phil Edmonds, *Australian convict* (ditto his wife, Frances); Neil Foster, *the 'Gutter' Press*; Bruce French, *Robin Hood*; David Gower, *Nazi S.S. officer*; Allan Lamb, *Fairy*; Jack Richards, *an Indian*; Wilf Slack, *Sailor*; Gladstone Small, *Arabian Knight*; James Whitaker, *Policeman*.

And for the management the list is: Peter Lush, *Queen's Counsel*; Micky Stewart, *Julius Caesar*; Lawrie Brown, *Errol Flynn*; Peter Austin (scorer), *Obscene Flasher*.

At about 10 p.m., Melbourne time, the whole team is mustered at its hotel for a BBC televised exchange of greetings, family to family, in the Noel Edmonds show back home on Christmas morning. I watch proceedings from the fringe, and bemoan the players' ill luck in having to wait around for God knows how long until the programme gets around to their contribution. All this late on, on the eve of the Test match. The Australian end of the TV enterprise can't even produce a decent big screen on which the players can observe their loved ones. And it is subsequently revealed by Peter Lush that the producer of the programme had fallen down on his promise to make England's participation the first item on the show, so that the boys could get a reasonably early night. The manager decides to file an official complaint to the BBC hierarchy. I think he is wholly justified in so doing.

December 26 (first day, Fourth Test)

My goodness, what a day for England, 95 for 1 at close of play after Australia, put in to bat, had been rattled out by Small and Botham for 141. Things are looking as good as they had done in Brisbane and now, as then, there is no great hurry for England to squeeze the trigger.

I suppose only Botham could mark his return to the Test match stage by taking 5 wickets for 41 runs in overdrive. It is probably a plus for England that, unable to bang it in short, he sets his mind to bowling straight, to a full length. The bounce of the pitch is even, the cloud cover encourages swing and there is some lateral movement for the seamers. We all know what can happen when Botham drops the odd one short. He has a remarkable gift for persuading batsmen to do something crass.

Two other England players play starring roles today. The second of them is Small who, admittedly in helpful conditions, makes the most of his opportunity with 5 for 48 – the first time he has taken as many in an innings during his short Test career. The third is Richards, with 5 catches. Three of them are brilliant ones, and he moves abreast of Jim Parks and Bob Taylor in the record books for England against Australia.

The English outcricket has been almost impeccable, what with persistently accurate bowling and some spectacular catches held. On the other side of the balance sheet, Australia rue a day in which at least half of their batsmen perish to bad shots or purely rash ones. To think that England have accomplished all this without Dilley, whose troublesome knee left him doubtful to last a five-day match. England, even on this Melbourne pitch, go for broke once more with a balanced attack. Foster is 12th man.

Early conditions call for Australian graft but they rush their fences. After Boon's departure in no time at all – caught off Small at slip – Marsh gives Richards his first exciting catch when attempting an uncharacteristic pull shot at Botham. Before long there is no question as to which of the sides has won the morning session. Border acquires many of his runs from the square cut, which can also cause his downfall. It does now, and we witness another fine catch by Richards off Botham.

In due course Botham takes another slip catch, a testing low one which he makes to look a simple matter, and Australia are 108 for 4. After that, the deluge: the last 7 are swept away for only 33 more.

Towards the end of the innings comes the best moment of all. Botham to McDermott, who hooks high, off the top edge, backward of square on the leg side. Broad is fielding deepish on the square boundary, Small likewise at fine. Richards sets off from behind the wicket, scampers more than 20 yards, and in spite of the converging presence of the two fielders – no distraction to a man with only one object in mind – takes as magnificent a catch of its kind as I have seen.

The only thing a crowd of almost 60,000 have cheered for patriotic reasons has been the news of Pat Cash moving towards a crucial singles victory in the Davis Cup Final against Sweden, at Kooyong down the road by the winding Yarra river. And, later, only the dismissal of Athey roused them, given out lbw to Reid after 58 had been raised for the first England wicket. Broad, comfortable, assured, and enjoying this Australian bowling, is 56 not out.

I wonder whether Gatting will now be joining 'Johnny Won't Hit Today' Douglas and David Gower (Edgbaston, 1985) as the only England captains in the history of the Ashes to have put Australia in to bat and then won the game.

It has also been a good day for the very popular and immensely respected correspondent of *The Times*. At a Lord's Taverners Boxing Day breakfast he has won the sweep. Rex Harrison has presented him with a cheque for more than 2,000 Australian dollars (about £1,000) for travel on Quantas.

December 27 (second day, Fourth Test)

From a highly encouraging pinnacle of 163 for 1 wicket England subside to an all out total of 349. Granted that 208 is a very adequate lead on first innings, but it really should have been a lot more. I have to report that the middle order didn't always bat with due care and attention.

No such words can be written of Broad who, by making a third hundred against Australia in successive Test matches, now stands in *Wisden* alongside the immortal Hobbs and Hammond. He has had himself a famous tour. We knew he was a good and brave player of fast bowling. Out here, against Matthews and Sleep, he has also proved himself a very competent performer against spin as well. He needed 233 balls to reach his hundred, in which he hit nine 4s. There was only one, fierce chance – to gulley off Hughes – when he was on 75.

But it's the captain who departs first today, having hooked the first ball of the afternoon directly to long leg, where Hughes accepts a good catch. Gatting has not been quite at his best in this innings. Broad goes next, caught behind off the admirable Reid for 112. It is a disappointment when Gower holes out to deep mid off, and even more so when Lamb, who has played some glittering shots on the off side, attempts another audacious one and becomes a further victim of Zoehrer. By then England are 251 for 5, the wickets slipping away.

For an hour and a half Botham plays with admirable restraint, notably when Sleep defensively comes round the wicket to him, bowling into the rough outside his leg stump. For most of the time the big man is content to thrust out an ample pad, but Border's ploy pays off. Running out of patience, Botham provides a third catch for Zoehrer when aiming a huge blow at Hughes. Then Richards goes, as he chips a simple catch off Reid to mid on, and so does DeFreitas. 289 for 8.

The ease with which Messrs. Emburey, Edmonds and Small then contribute 60 off the new ball for the last two wickets merely emphasises how many more England might have made if some of their betters hadn't been in so much of a hurry. Reid has a deserved 4 for 78. McDermott is fortunate to take 4 for 83, three of his wickets being tail enders. But I think Australia's bowlers and catchers have had their best day in the series.

December 28 (third day, Fourth Test)

What a day it has been! Australia bowled out for 194, victory for England by an innings and 14 runs, Ashes retained and series won. It's 2–0 and one to play. That lead of 208 was more than adequate.

It has been a day when the bounce is somewhat lower and there is just enough movement off the seam now and again to keep the quicker bowlers on the *qui vive*. But it is England's spinners who enjoy the last laugh. They share five of the last seven Australian wickets which fall for 41 runs. The other two are run outs.

But back to the start of it all when Small, in a fine opening spell down the breeze, has Boon attempting to leave a ball alone but edging it to Gatting at slip. Boon's seventh miserable score in eight innings this series. Australia are 48 for 1 when DeFreitas, now with the wind behind him in a second spell, persuades Jones to cut when cramped for room. That means a sharper slip catch for England's captain.

Next, a key prize, that of Border, who has looked in ominously good fettle. He drives at Small, and Emburey takes a very hot slip catch indeed, high to his right hand side. Does he ever drop anything? It had certainly made for riveting cricket as Marsh and Border added 65 for the third wicket.

Emburey and Edmonds are calling the shots by mid-afternoon. Emburey appears incensed to be denied a catch by Athey standing close in to Marsh, who then conveniently runs himself out. From this point onwards Australian spectators have nothing to get excited about except a view of Pat Cash winning the vital Davis Cup rubber against Sweden on the big television screen. Matthews plays on to Emburey. Sleep is run out thanks to Gower's speedy pickup and throw and the legerdemain of Edmonds, who pulls the ball down and hits the stumps. Two hot chances have gone astray off Emburey before the spinners briskly work their way through Waugh, whose combative 49 lasts more than an hour and a half, and then through nine, ten, jack. At exactly 4.39 p.m. Hughes heaves Edmonds to long leg, Small throws the ball aloft and England are entitled to let their hair down.

Mike Gatting has joined the list of England captains – Percy Chapman (1928/29), Len Hutton (1954/55) and Mike Brearley (1978/79) – who have retained the Ashes in Australia this century. It is the first time England have won a Test Match inside three days in this country since A. C. MacLaren's side did just that, in Sydney, in 1901/02.

Gatting says afterwards that he was never in doubt about putting Australia in to bat. 'We got the early wickets we needed today, and we held our catches. It was touch and go between Small and Foster to take Dilley's place. Gladstone certainly delivered the goods.' I think that in saying this he was making a nice public gesture to Foster. Anyway, Small has certainly come up trumps, and he becomes the third Englishman after Botham (First Test) and Broad (Second) to win the Benson and Hedges man of the match award.

Border declares afterwards that he wanted Ritchie to play. 'You can't go into a Test Match with only four specialist batsmen.' Captain at odds with his selectors? Gatting is equally surprised, but gratified, by his opponents' selection. 'I feel pretty numb,' Border adds, 'but not as low as I did after we lost in Brisbane. We've simply got to hang in somehow, and I'm determined to see it out.' He has now led Australia through 14 Test Matches without a single win.

December 29

Two days off: welcome relief for players denied much time to relax by what I think is the most demanding schedule ever devised for an England team touring this country. Less of it for media at daily behest of their lords and masters back

FOURTH TEST

Melbourne, 26–28 December 1986

AUSTRALIA

	1st innings		2nd innings	
G. R. Marsh	c Richards b Botham	17	run out	60
D. C. Boon	c Botham b Small	7	c Gatting b Small	8
D. M. Jones	c Gower b Small	59	c Gatting b DeFreitas	21
A. R. Border*	c Richards b Botham	15	c Emburey b Small	34
S. R. Waugh	c Botham b Small	10	b Edmonds	49
G. R. J. Matthews	c Botham b Small	14	b Emburey	0
P. R. Sleep	c Richards b Small	0	run out	6
T. J. Zoehrer†	b Botham	5	c Athey b Edmonds	1
C. J. McDermott	c Richards b Botham	0	b Emburey	1
M. G. Hughes	c Richards b Botham	2	c Small b Edmonds	8
B. A. Reid	not out	2	not out	0
Extras	(b 2, lb 1, w 1, nb 7)	10	(lb 3, w 1, nb 2)	6
TOTAL		141		194

Fall of wickets: 16, 44, 80, 108, 118, 118, 129, 133, 137.
Second innings: 13, 48, 113, 153, 153, 179, 180, 189, 189.

Bowling: Small 22.4-7-48-5; DeFreitas 11-1-30-0; Emburey 4-0-16-0; Botham 16-4-41-5; Gatting 1-0-4-0.
Second innings: DeFreitas 12-1-44-1; Small 15-3-40-2; Botham 7-1-19-0; Edmonds 19.4-5-45-3; Emburey 20-5-43-2.

ENGLAND

	1st innings	
B. C. Broad	c Zoehrer b Hughes	112
C. W. J. Athey	lbw b Reid	21
M. W. Gatting*	c Hughes b Reid	40
A. J. Lamb	c Zoehrer b Reid	43
D. I. Gower	c Matthews b Sleep	7
I. T. Botham	c Zoehrer b McDermott	29
C. J. Richards†	c Marsh b Reid	3
P. A. J. DeFreitas	c Matthews b McDermott	7
J. E. Emburey	c&b McDermott	22
P. H. Edmonds	lbw b McDermott	19
G. C. Small	not out	21
Extras	(b 6, lb 7, w 1, nb 11)	25
TOTAL		349

Fall of wickets: 58, 163, 198, 219, 251, 273, 277, 289, 319.

Bowling: McDermott 26.5-4-83-4; Hughes 30-3-94-1; Reid 28-5-78-4; Waugh 8-4-16-0; Sleep 28-4-65-1.

Toss: England.
Umpires: A. R. Crafter and R. A. French.

home. However, the local press provide some handy headlines for comment. 'Shameful capitulation', 'Selectors a flop, too', and even 'Can Pat Cash bat or bowl?' are some of them. Bill O'Reilly thunders away in his syndicated column about sacking the Australian selectors as soon as the series is finished, and giving Allan Border the boot, too.

Axing the selectors, who have made some curious decisions, is one thing, giving Border the heave-ho quite another. Quite simply, there is no obvious successor to him in sight. Australia should be grateful that a man who must feel like Atlas, with the weight of the world on his shoulders, still wants to see it through.

The Australian manager had his squad in the nets again today, as he did on Christmas Day, but alas virtue is not always rewarded. I reflect that it says very little for the present quality of Australian cricket, in technical as well as temperamental terms, that they should have been trounced by an England side without their main strike bowler, Graham Dilley, and with Ian Botham on something less than full throttle. It was splendid to see Gladstone Small, a popular, ever cheerful member of the party, taking his chance so well. He will now press very strongly for the place of Phillip DeFreitas in Sydney.

He was fortunate of course to operate on what, right to the end of the game, was essentially a seamer's pitch. You wouldn't have thought so, seeing Australia batting so ineptly against our two spinners.

Mike Gatting has led from the front on this tour and, surely with shrewd support from Micky Stewart, has done a sound tactical job overall. To hear him say that he wasn't enjoying the captaincy job in general terms was certainly a surprise, and I can only assume that some of the pressures off the field have got him down. They would have been a lot more stringent if his team had been losing. It has been clear throughout the series so far that there has been one man in charge on the field. The same could not always have been said in recent years. The captain had a skin outwardly thick enough to shrug off the public rebuke he got from his manager. He is learning, as a bluff, down-the-middle, likeable character, to speak his mind at media conferences and to utter something more forthright and interesting. Things are beginning to hum again for England's cricket, not before time, and I simply hope that the captain will come to enjoy his job in almost all of its aspects.

Old England cricketers continue to put in an appearance, some of them as 'masters of ceremonies', conducting tours from home. Mike Denness is one of them, though I haven't bumped into him yet, John Snow another. Geoff Boycott is now also with us, contributing his thoughts for the *Daily Mail*. These are written for him by our equable tour leader, Peter Smith, an old pro much liked and respected by all. But even he doesn't know where Boycott is staying. The great man is incommunicado. On non-playing days he telephones at agreed times from a number not even revealed to his writer. A strange man is our Geoffrey.

Another telex from the desk, this time from Assistant Sportsed, enjoining me to keep my eyes open, as from January 1, for Botham/Worcestershire developments. This calls for what I think is yet another tactful rejoinder, on the lines that any hard news on the subject will be first revealed by Chris Lander in the *Sun*, to which I.B. is contracted. So perhaps it would be best for the London end to be even more attentive?

December 30

The affable, helpful captain provides the scribes, 'ere we all fly back to Perth again, with his thoughts on the Benson and Hedges Challenge tournament in which England play their first game, against Australia on New Year's Day. 'We've accomplished the main job, retaining the Ashes and winning the series,' he says. 'Now I've got a motivation job to do, to make sure we're all in the right frame of mind and keep the pressure on Australia. We've all got to take this showpiece thing very seriously, and we'll go in with our strongest side.' That means Graham Dilley being added to the 11 who trounced Australia in the Melbourne Test, a decision about whom to leave out being left until the morning of the match. 'Graham,' the captain adds, 'still has some fluid on his knee but he's probably as fit now as he'll be for the rest of the tour.'

England are required to name a squad of 14 players by tomorrow evening, and seem certain to omit Bruce French and Wilf Slack, two loyal members of the party whose tour is slipping away from them fast. I shall feel very sorry for both of them.

The skipper believes that the biggest obstacle his side has to overcome when taking on the West Indies is a mental one. However, as we learn when nearing Perth, Pakistan have done England and Australia a service, beating the favourites, in the first (day/night) game of the tournament today, by 34 runs.

I am tempted, as I report for the paper, to suggest that a pyjama game bonanza like this, coming hard between the Fourth and Fifth Test Matches, is an absurd piece of scheduling. I wonder what the reaction of *both* sides would have been had the series stood at one-all after Melbourne and they then, before going to Sydney for its climax, had to divert themselves into a totally different kind of game to link in with the America's Cup. As it happens, of course, the Sydney Test, in Davis Cup terms, is a dead rubber. The Australian public, no great supporters of losing teams, are unlikely to have Sydney cricket ground bursting at the seams. It appears that the overall income generated by the England tour is already 20 per cent down on projected figures. The loss of two days' play in the Fourth Test was no help to local treasurers. So the 'one-off' competition now being staged in Perth will undoubtedly produce some handy dollars for the Australian Cricket Board, as well as for Kerry Packer's PBL marketing company, which does a highly professional job. But just how bananas Australian cricket has gone over the abbreviated game is revealed by the fact that when Allan Border plays against us in two days' time, it will be his 139th one-day international. Thank heavens the TCCB back home have had the good sense, in international terms, to preserve a proper balance between the two kinds of cricket.

On the flight westwards I observe that Allan Lamb and Graham Dilley are still sporting their rather smart, black-ribboned straw hats. Dilley never seems to take his off, indoors or out. I wonder whether he goes to bed in it. Perhaps he has been watching too many of those old Humphrey Bogart/George Raft films.

December 31

Peace, perfect peace: no paper to file for this evening. I spend most of the day by the splendid pool at the Merlin hotel, soaking up the sunshine and repairing a tan not well provided for in recent weeks. The sheer effort of it is so tiring that I need to retire to my room for a ziz before a party of scribes celebrate the new year at a local restaurant. We get a far more civilised deal than Chris Lander and Graham Otway, who make the mistake of joining the teeming roisterers in Fremantle and find the whole place has run out of booze.

January 1 1987 (Perth Challenge preliminary v. Australia)

England have started their Benson and Hedges Challenge on the right note with a comfortable win over Australia by 37 runs. They rustle up the commanding total of 272 for 6 after Gatting has won the toss (Broad 76, Athey 34, Botham 66, Lamb 68), and even an exciting 104 from Dean Jones – off only 125 balls – can't take Australia within range. A ground record crowd of more than 27,000 – about twice as many as on any day of the Second Test Match here – watch Australia go down under the new floodlights. Those who detest the pyjama game can't argue with a figure like that.

The pitch is benign, the outfield lightning fast, and England get away to a splendid start, 86 for the first wicket in 22 overs. Mission more or less completed, Athey then gets himself out. Broad is moving along beautifully when he is run out, whereupon Botham in another remarkable innings thunders his way to 68 off just 39 balls, including 26 off Davis in one over. He begins it with two straight 4s hit with enormous power, and finishes with a vast 6 over long on, plus another over extra cover. Lamb is no slouch either, making 66 off 72 balls. In their 10 overs together, the England score advances by 106.

In Australia's reply Boon is soon accounted for when he hits DeFreitas straight to Emburey, one of two gullies posted specially for him by Gatting. The English outcricket is businesslike, sometimes brilliant, all through – and certainly there is nothing more shining than a catch made by Emburey at long on, when Australia have mounted a despairing flurry. Macleay lofts Dilley high towards the boundary. The ball appears to be clearing Emburey when, leaping up and backwards, he grasps the ball with one arm outstretched and still retains control of it though falling in a heap. Emburey has clung on to some great catches this tour, but none better than this.

Phillip DeFreitas makes an interesting comment to me afterwards. 'When I started bowling, I never felt such butterflies in my life. The atmosphere under those lights really got to me. I think Gladstone (Small) must have felt the same.'

The Lord's hierarchy are now with us, as official guests – and rightly so – of the Australian Board. A. C. (Alan) Smith joined up in Melbourne. Newly appointed chief executive of the Test and County Cricket Board, he takes over officially today from the long-serving, highly respected secretary, Donald Carr, who has come out here with Raman Subba Row (TCCB chairman) and Jack Bailey, secretary of

MCC and of the International Cricket Conference. Another official guest is J. J. (John) Warr, who apart from representing Australian interests on the ICC back home is without question one of the most brilliant after-dinner speakers I have known. He used, long ago, to write some very amusing features for *The Sunday Telegraph*. It was the readers' loss when he stopped producing them.

We have also been joined by Alec Bedser, who turned up in Melbourne, and by Trevor Bailey, appearing for the first time in Perth. Alec has always had a soft spot for Australia, something the Australians reciprocate in their respect for a great bowler who has served the game unselfishly as an England selector for donkey's years. The Aussies used to hate Bailey's guts, so often did his batting obstruct their best endeavours. But as with Bedser, they knew a fine competitor when they saw one.

January 2

Last evening, in addition to my match report, I filed another piece about Botham and Worcestershire, Graham Dilley and Kent, and the cancellation of Australia's tour to West Indies in early 1988. It was getting on for midnight when – these jobs completed – I hit the hay. It had been a long day.

Telephone call from Sportsed at 1.30 a.m. is not the best start to a new one. Could I follow up the Australian tour story with quotes from various officials here? At this time of night? I enquire. Does he seriously think that I should wake them up? At this point the lines goes dead, someone having pulled the plug. Sportsed probably thinks it was me. On reflection, I wish it had been.

England have the day off while Australian cricket hits a new low. Pakistan win by 1 wicket, off the penultimate ball of their innings, in a dramatic climax not envisaged after Australia had made 273 for 6 wickets. How Australia failed to defend such a substantial score only they can tell. Allan Border is not available for comment afterwards, which is no

BENSON AND HEDGES
PERTH CHALLENGE PRELIMINARY

1 January 1987

ENGLAND

B. C. Broad	run out	76
C. W. J. Athey	c Zoehrer b O'Donnell	34
D. I. Gower	c Zoehrer b Whitney	6
A. J. Lamb	c Zoehrer b Reid	66
I. T. Botham	c Zoehrer b Waugh	68
M. W. Gatting*	not out	5
C. J. Richards†	c Border b Reid	4
P. A. J. DeFreitas	not out	0
Extras	(b 2, lb 6, w 4, nb 1)	13
TOTAL (for 6 wkts, 49 overs)		272

Did not bat: J. E. Emburey, G. R. Dilley, G. C. Small.

Fall of wickets: 86, 95, 150, 256, 262, 271.

Bowling: Davis 8-1-48-0; Whitney 10-0-56-1; Macleay 9-0-51-0; Reid 10-1-46-2; O'Donnell 7-0-39-1; Waugh 5-0-24-1.

AUSTRALIA

G. R. Marsh	b Botham	28
D. C. Boon	c Emburey b DeFreitas	1
D. M. Jones	c Gower b Dilley	104
A. R. Border*	b Emburey	26
S. R. Waugh	c Richards b Small	16
S. P. O'Donnell	run out	0
K. H. Macleay	c Emburey b Dilley	21
T. J. Zoehrer†	c Botham b DeFreitas	1
M. R. Whitney	run out	6
B. A. Reid	b DeFreitas	10
S. P. Davis	not out	1
Extras	(lb 7, w 10, nb 4)	21
TOTAL (all out, 48.2 overs)		235

Fall of wickets: 7, 50, 125, 149, 158, 210, 214, 217, 233.

Bowling: DeFreitas 9.2-0-42-3; Dilley 10-1-31-2; Botham 10-0-52-1; Small 9-0-62-1; Emburey 10-0-41-1.

surprise. He is once again like Atlas with the weight of the world on his shoulders. His bowlers have been thrashed to all parts by the Pakistan tail. But all credit to the winners, who slump in mid-order, after a quite brilliant opening fusillade from Qasim Omar, but keep up a difficult chase with great panache. A jubilant Imran Khan says afterwards that in all his time in his national side he has never known such a splendid team spirit. I advise readers back home to note the name Qasim, who was born in Kenya. Of its kind, his innings today is as exciting as any I have seen this Australian summer. Viv Richards could play with no greater mastery.

Pakistan's second win in the round-robin preliminaries virtually puts them through to the final. If England lose to the West Indies tomorrow, they could still reach the last round by beating Pakistan in their third game. Pakistan might not be too sorry to lose that one if by so doing they avoid meeting West Indies in the final.

I am infuriated to hear during the day that my story about Australia not going to West Indies next year (which was put my way by a kindly Jack Bannister) appeared in today's *Telegraph* under someone else's name. I wonder what further intolerable things are in store from the sports desk before my tour is out. I ring Sportsed at 3 p.m. GMT but he is still out at lunch. Then I hear he has sent me a telex – to the wrong hotel. Having gone to collect it at about midnight, I find he would still welcome reaction from various Board officials on significance of tour cancellation. I send the following reply on Tandy: 'Can I suggest that whoever had the by-line over my story does his own research by way of follow up?'

January 3 (Perth Challenge preliminary v. West Indies)

It's not often these days that England enjoy a victory over West Indies – even in the limited overs game. But they manage an exciting one now, by 19 runs. England 228 for 9 (Lamb 71, Richards 50), West Indies all out 209.

Dilley, hostile and accurate, virtually seals the result with a devastating second spell after Logie and Dujon's partnership of 74 for the fifth wicket has taken West Indies within 51 runs of success. He rips out 4 wickets for 7 runs in only 19 balls, a performance which rightly wins him the man of the match award from Ian Chappell.

Gatting has some problems with his bowling changes. Edmonds is relatively expensive on this occasion, though no more so than Harper has been for West Indies. One of the limited-over regulations in Australia demands that for the first 15 overs of an innings seven fielders, two of them stationary within 15 yards of the bat, must be inside the semi-circled lines. It would be a risky business, therefore, to introduce a spin bowler too early. However, in due course Emburey tightens the screw.

Emburey, Edmonds and Small all contribute sensibly after Lamb has played his best knock on a major occasion during this expedition. He is simply exuding confidence again. Perth clearly brings out the best in Richards. This is where he got his Test hundred. It is a staunch effort to make a presentable total after losing Broad for 0, Athey for 1, and Gower for 11. A nasty start indeed against Big Joel and Marshall, but nothing new in that.

I report for my paper another one-day regulation reading thus: 'If the ball passes or would have passed above the shoulder height of the striker standing in his normal batting stance at the crease, either umpire shall call and signal "No Ball".' The English regulation is phrased slightly differently: 'If the ball passes over head-height of the striker standing upright at the crease, the umpire shall call and signal "Wide".' I think Australia's rule is the better one, and suggest as much to Raman Subba Row, chairman of the TCCB. He agrees that they should have another look at their own version.

BENSON AND HEDGES
PERTH CHALLENGE PRELIMINARY

3 January 1987

ENGLAND

B. C. Broad	c Garner b Marshall	0
C. W. J. Athey	c Richardson b Garner	1
D. I. Gower	c Dujon b Garner	11
A. J. Lamb	c Harper b Marshall	71
M. W. Gatting*	c Garner b Walsh	15
I. T. Botham	c Greenidge b Harper	11
C. J. Richards†	c Dujon b Garner	50
J. E. Emburey	c Harper b Garner	18
P. H. Edmonds	not out	16
G. R. Dilley	c&b Garner	1
G. C. Small	not out	8
Extras	(lb 10, w 8, nb 8)	26
TOTAL (for 9 wkts, 50 overs)		228

Fall of wickets: 3, 10, 35, 67, 96, 156, 194, 209, 211.

Bowling: Marshall 10-1-23-2; Garner 10-0-47-5; Holding 10-0-33-0; Walsh 9-0-40-1; Harper 10-0-63-1; Richards 1-0-5-0.

WEST INDIES

G. C. Greenidge	b Small	20
D. L. Haynes	lbw b Small	4
R. B. Richardson	c Gatting b Botham	12
I. V. A. Richards*	c Broad b Emburey	45
A. L. Logie	c Richards b Dilley	51
P. J. L. Dujon†	b Dilley	36
R. A. Harper	run out	4
M. D. Marshall	b Dilley	7
M. A. Holding	c Edmonds b Dilley	7
J. Garner	not out	4
C. A. Walsh	lbw b Emburey	0
Extras	(b 4, lb 9, w 4, nb 2)	19
TOTAL (all out, 48.2 overs)		209

Fall of wickets: 9, 39, 51, 104, 178, 187, 187, 201, 208.

Bowling: Dilley 10-0-46-4; Small 10-1-37-2; Botham 10-1-29-1; Edmonds 9-1-53-0; Emburey 9.2-0-31-2.

January 4

Although it will be England against Pakistan in the final, 22,000 customers still turn up to watch Australia and West Indies playing for third place. They see Australia relentlessly bowled out for 91, to lose by 164 runs. Their side has now lost all three of their round-robin games. Add to this their loss of the Test series, and supporters here may think that things can't get much worse.

I feel sorry for Australia's batsmen today, facing a very determined battery of fast bowlers, the first two of them, Garner and Gray, banging it down short of a length from a great height – on a pitch, moreover, providing enough bounce, not always even, to whet their appetites. After twelve overs they had struggled to 18 for 3, Marsh having been hit in the throat by Garner. Even a great player like Border can make only 3 off 9 overs and 9 off 13 altogether. Quite simply it is no contest. With a brave 28 Waugh is the only man to reach double figures. Garner takes 3 for 10 and Gray, more remarkably, has 3 for 9 off 7.4 overs.

All this after West Indies have made 255 for 8 with a fine hundred by Greenidge and nothing much from anyone else except Holding, who thrashes 53 off 35 balls at the climax to leave a much better batting side than Australia under a lot of pressure.

Allan Border says afterwards that Australia were still stunned by their defeat at the hands of Pakistan, when the game slid away from them in the closing stages. 'The boys have been given three days off,' he adds, 'and in their present mood it would probably be best if they went on the beach and turned up in time for the final Test in Sydney.' I think he is right; they need a break. Border also complained that the umpires had not invoked, often enough, the local regulation about short-pitched bowling. I think he is right on that one, too.

Yet another failure by Boon, in what must have been his last chance, has to cry finis to his place in the Test side. I fancy that McDermott has said goodbye again to his. His first two overs – after Reid and Macleay had bowled a very restrictive spell against Greenidge and Haynes – went for 25 runs. It is control that Australia's bowlers need in the final Test. I would pick Macleay to open with Reid.

At the end of the day we are all generously invited to a barbecue by the Western Australian cricket journalists: a splendidly informal party which I leave early in order to be on time at Perth airport for the arrival of Pauline, the last, I think, of the wives, girl friends and what-have-you to join the English camp. We have not seen each other for almost three months, so it is a joyous reunion. She is staying on until the end of the tour, after which we plan a week up at the Great Barrier Reef which, I have always told myself, I must see 'ere slipping off this mortal coil.

January 5 (Perth Challenge preliminary v. Pakistan)

Yet another win for England and a hectic one at that. Chasing a target of 230, after Pakistan had won the toss and batted first, they seem to be coasting home at 156 for 2 but then subside to 208 for 7 in the 47th over. However, Emburey is an old hand in a crisis of this sort, and DeFreitas looks one, too, as they steer their side to victory by 3 wickets with 2 balls remaining.

All this follows 97 from Broad, 42 from Athey, who surrenders his wicket after doing his duty in an opening partnership of 104, and a rousing 32 by Lamb. Unfortunately, Lamb holes out prematurely in the deep, and so does Botham. Gatting and Richards fall cheaply to spectacular run outs. One way and another, England put themselves under unnecessary final pressure.

The unluckiest batsman today is Broad, who is adjudged caught behind off Imran when the TV replay clearly reveals that it had hit his pad, some distance from the bat.

There is another failure by Gower, his scores in this bonanza now being 6, 11 and 2. His last Test innings was 7, in Melbourne. I dare say he may bat like a prince again in the final Test. I wish England had given Whitaker a chance in a match which is merely a dress rehearsal for the final between the same two sides. However, they have given Dilley a rest, omitted Edmonds, and included DeFreitas and Foster. DeFreitas bowls an excellent line and length but poor Foster has to go off with a knee injury after sending down 4 overs for 23.

There is one highly unusual and, as it transpires, illegal dismissal. Umpire French rules Rameez run out off a no ball from Gatting, but Law 38 (2) holds that a striker cannot be dismissed in this way unless he is attempting a run. Rameez certainly is not.

· The end of Pakistan's innings is distinguished by Javed Miandad, who gives Emburey some stick and makes 59 off 65 balls. I am sure that England must start the final as favourites. Pakistan have a problem finding a fifth bowler.

January 6

When Australia select their Test sides, the Board release the news alternatively to suit Australian morning and evening newspapers. It being now the turn of the evenings, the side for Sydney is embargoed until, I think, 5.30 a.m. eastern seaboard time, which is 2.30 a.m. in Perth. I have arranged with the ever helpful David Lloyd, of the Press Association, who never seems to stop working, that he should ring me with the details at a rather inconvenient hour. This he does, and I then compose a short piece for today's paper in England, arriving for Sportsed at about 8.15 p.m. GMT, in ample time to catch most editions.

The much criticised Australian selectors seem due for further local stick. Boon and McDermott, predictably, are left out of their 12 man squad. In come Dirk Wellham and Peter Taylor of New South Wales, and there is only one specialist opening batsman, Geoff Marsh, left in their side.

BENSON AND HEDGES
PERTH CHALLENGE PRELIMINARY

5 January 1987

PAKISTAN

Qasim Omar	b Botham	32
Shoaib Mohammad	c DeFreitas b Emburey	66
Rameez Raja	run out	15
Javed Miandad	c Athey b Emburey	59
Imran Khan*	c Gower b DeFreitas	23
Manzoor Elahi	not out	9
Wasim Akram	not out	1
Extras	(lb 15, w 1, nb 8)	24
TOTAL (5 wkts, 50 overs)		229

Did not bat: Mudassar Nazar, Asif Mujtaba, Salim yousuf, Salim Jaffer.

Fall of wickets: 61, 98, 156, 198, 225.

Bowling: DeFreitas 9-1-24-1; Small 10-0-41-0; Foster 4-0-23-0; Botham 10-1-37-1; Gatting 7-0-24-0; Emburey 10-0-65-2.

ENGLAND

B. C. Broad	c Salim Yousuf b Imran	97
C. W. J. Athey	b Manzoor Elahi	42
D. I. Gower	c Shoaib b Mudassar	2
A. J. Lamb	c Javed b Shoaib	32
I. T. Botham	c Rameez b Wasim Akram	10
M. W. Gatting*	run out	7
C. J. Richards†	run out	0
P. A. J. DeFreitas	not out	13
J. E. Emburey	not out	11
Extras	(b 1, lb 13, w 3, nb 1)	18
TOTAL (for 7 wkts 49.4 overs)		232

Did not bat: N. A. Foster, G. C. Small.

Fall of wickets: 104, 108, 156, 184, 199, 204, 208.

Bowling: Wasim Akram 9.4-1-28-1; Salim Jaffer 10-2-43-0; Imran Khan 9-0-41-1; Mudassar Nazar 10-0-39-1; Asif Mujtaba 3-0-19-0; Manzoor Elahi 3-0-24-1; Shoaib Mohammad 5-0-24-1.

Surprisingly, Greg Matthews is retained, and it will please England if he plays. But they must include two spinners in Sydney, Peter Sleep plus one other. Matthews or Taylor, then, for 12th man. Taylor is an off-break bowler who made his Sheffield Shield debut last season here.

I have had an answer from Sir Donald Bradman: 'Dear Peter, To be a sports editor one has to be optimistic. The one from the D.T. is no exception. I'm sure he is well aware of my attitude towards press statements. A couple of my colleagues have gone into print in the last few days, but I feel they have done nothing for the game or the players and have not improved their own reputations. Having left the scene completely I prefer to leave matters to current administrators, players and the press, and therefore I'm sorry I can't agree to your requests. Hope you had a good Xmas and that 1987 will be kind. Yours sincerely. (signed) Don Bradman.'

Well, I was right about that one. I send it on Tandy to Sportsed, without comment.

Benson and Hedges Challenge dinner at the Sheraton, a big, dinner-jacketed 'do' attended by all four teams, which UK media representatives are charitably allowed to attend in lounge suits. The custom in Australia, at this sort of function, is to have a master of ceremonies, in this case Ian Wooldridge, who introduces speakers between the various courses. This gets things over and done with rather sooner than at home, but if you have to endure a long-drawn-out oration after the sole *bonne femme* it tends to have you straining to see the *filet mignon*. Official speeches in Australia seem to be even more boring than those in UK. Happily, J. J. Warr is on the toast list, which elevates the entire proceedings. He is Australia's representative in England on the International Cricket Conference.

This dinner has one feature I heartily endorse: the loyal toast to Her Majesty the Queen is drunk almost as soon as the meal is first served. I have never thought that this traditional toast is any less loyal for being drunk early. It enables those who so desire to enjoy their inter-course smoking.

I learn at this dinner that Geoff Marsh has been named as vice-captain of Australia, in succession to David Boon, for the final Test. It is said that the Australian selectors unanimously wanted Dirk Wellham, captain of New South Wales, to fill that office but were over-ruled by the Australian Cricket Board. Do the selectors want another, proven captain in their side as a potential successor to Allan Border in the event of another Australian debacle in Sydney? Do the Board not want as vice-captain someone who at one time got himself involved with a 'rebel' tour of South Africa but subsequently withdrew from it? And who will open Australia's innings with Marsh? Wellham has never gone in first in a first-class match. It will, I suppose, be Greg Ritchie, who is certainly a good enough batsman to make a success of an unfamiliar role.

There is also a splendid rumour going the rounds that the Australian Board invited the wrong Taylor (Mark) of New South Wales. Mark is an opening batsman, Peter (the selectors' choice) a 30-year-old off spinner with only six first-class games under his belt, one of them his only Sheffield Shield game this summer. 'Peter who?' the scribes have enquired.

All this makes useful material for Sportsed, as well as some reflections on England ringing their till with all the win money they are collecting. I calculate that to this point they have earned themselves, from Benson and Hedges here, or from Cornhill Insurance in England, something like £13,000 for team and individual performances. Another £10,000 odd is due if they win tomorrow's final. When the Benson and Hedges prize money for drawn Test matches is divided, two-thirds of it to the winners of the series, further handy amounts will be forthcoming. The winners of the Benson and Hedges World Series Cup, to be staged in January/February, will annex more than £15,000. I wonder what some of the old professionals, who had to rub along on a pittance, think about it all.

January 7 (Perth Challenge Final v. Pakistan)

No real problem at all. England coast home by 5 wickets and a spectacular cascade of fireworks in a blue, blue sky – what a marvellous climate they have in Perth – greets the winning smash from Ian Botham. Mike Gatting can't have been sorry to win the toss. He puts Pakistan in, and they struggle all the way against some splendid outcricket to make only 166 for 9. It would have been a lot less but for a masterful display by Javed Miandad who holds the whole piece together and contrives, during a last wicket partnership, to receive 49 of the balls sent down and thus to ensure that his side last the 50-over course.

The final is played on the bouncier of the two pitches prepared for this tournament. It was watered two days earlier. England's quick bowlers present some distinctly fiery problems, Dilley being outstanding and DeFreitas not far behind him. Botham bowls a steady 10-over stint right through, and takes 3 wickets, some from strokes of sheer desperation when Pakistan were behind the clock. Small nips in with 3 wickets for very little, and Pakistan subside from 127 for 5 to 131 for 9. But Javed finishes with 77 not out, and Rod Marsh later gets it right when naming him man of the match. Without him, there would scarcely have been one.

There are some early hiccoughs when England begin their reply: Athey and Broad depart for 1 and 0 respectively – Broad to a bad decision from the same umpire, Dick French, for the second time in consecutive matches. This time, he is given out caught behind when the TV replay reveals that the ball merely brushed his hip. Unfortunately, Broad, in stepping away from the crease, gives French the impression that he is on his way home, 'walking' as we say. So French raises his digit. But in spite of this it is nice to hear Gatting say afterwards that he has no complaint about the umpiring out here. He says he thinks the adjudicating in the Test series has been very good. It is of course what losing captains have to say that sometimes makes for more quotable stuff.

Gower looks pretty good again until he whacks a ball straight into the hands of cover point, right off the middle of the bat. Then Lamb and Gatting, the skipper after an unpromising start, push England firmly on the road with a partnership of 89. He says later that losing two early wickets was unfortunate 'but we weren't chasing 230.'

At the end of it all Gatting observes that the support from English spectators had been tremendous (he is much addicted to that word). I think their continual mindless chanting is a pain in the arse for their Australian hosts, and anything England's captain can do to discourage it would be a bonus. What is more, half of England's side, the Benson and Hedges trophy held aloft, cross the ground to parade it, Cup Final fashion, in front of noisy, well-oiled adherents. I must add, as counter-balance to these doubtless old-fashioned thoughts, that the local police thought this gesture helped to restrain many more of those supporters from rushing on to the arena and snarling things up. Those who do so are ruthlessly felled by some splendid rugby tackles.

It has been another long day, or at least it seems like it after being up in the small hours. We return to our hotel after a farewell dinner with David and Ann Haultain, who have ensured these past two days that Pauline could relax, recovering from jet lag, at their home close to Fremantle, by the Swan river. The telephone rings just after I have hit the hay. Midnight nears. Sportsed again. Would I care to file ten or so paras on the Australian Board's official announcement about the cancellation of their tour in the West Indies? Might it not be more suitable, I enquire, if the man whose by-line appeared on my original story now did another one? Ah, but Nigel Dudley is now in India, I am told. In that case, I say, let somebody else do it.

BENSON AND HEDGES
PERTH CHALLENGE FINAL

7 January 1987

PAKISTAN

Qasim Omar	c Broad b Botham	21
Shoaib Mohammad	b Dilley	0
Rameez Raja	c Athey b Botham	22
Javed Miandad	not out	77
Asif Mujtaba	c Gower b Botham	7
Imran Khan*	c Richards b Gatting	5
Manzoor Elahi	c Gower b Small	20
Salim Yousuf†	c Athey b Small	0
Mudassar Nazar	c Gower b Emburey	0
Wasim Akram	c Gatting b Small	2
Salim Jaffer	not out	3
Extras	(lb 5, w 1, nb 3)	9
TOTAL (50 overs, 9 wkts)		166

Fall of wickets: 2, 36, 58, 76, 89, 127, 127, 128, 131.

Bowling: DeFreitas 10-1-33-0; Dilley 10-0-23-1; Botham 10-2-24-3; Small 10-0-28-3; Emburey 8-0-34-1; Gatting 2-0-14-1.

ENGLAND

B. C. Broad	c Yousuf b Akram	0
C. W. J. Athey	c Yousuf b Imran	1
D. I. Gower	c Shoaib b Imran	31
A. J. Lamb	c Yousuf b Akram	47
M. W. Gatting*	b Akram	49
I. T. Botham	not out	23
C. J. Richards†	not out	7
Extras	(lb 8, w 1)	9
TOTAL (40.1 overs, 5 wkts)		167

Did not bat: P. A. J. DeFreitas, J. E. Emburey, G. R. Dilley, G. C. Small.

Fall of wickets: 1, 7, 47, 136, 145.

Bowling: Imran Khan 8-2-30-2; Wasim Akram 10-2-27-3; Salim Jaffer 10-1-43-0; Mudassar Nazar 5.1-0-22-0; Shoaib Mohammad 2-0-11-0; Manzoor Elahi 5-0-26-0.

January 8

I think we are all sorry to be saying farewell to the fair city of Perth, which is blessed by one of the finest climates in the world. We haven't seen a cloud for days. But I dare say none of us regrets that this is the last close-on four-hour flight across the continent.

I chat with Allan Lamb, amongst other things, about his ambitions in Sydney – his last chance, after a poor run of scores in the series, to get his first Test hundred overseas. 'Christ,' he says, 'I'm suffering from a long drought, and I'd give my eye teeth to make it.' He has certainly been in splendid nick in the one-day games in Perth. He has never really been out of touch all tour but has fallen too often and too early to impatience. He just likes to get on with it, and play his natural, forceful game.

The flight is nearing Sydney when the captain comes through on inter-com.: 'Wake up, Michael. We're beginning our descent now.' Shades of the captain's lie-in in Melbourne. I don't doubt for one moment that the irrepressibly buoyant 'Lamby' has put the skipper up to it.

I have also had a word with Liam, son of Ian Botham, who is showing all the signs of developing into a remarkable games player. I ask him about his top score at cricket. '164 not out,' he replies, quite modestly. With ten 4s and four 6s, it appears. That's tremendous stuff for a nine-year-old who, in spite of his father's fame, seems a very nice lad, feet on the floor and a credit to his parents.

January 9

In Sydney for the first time and at long last, after almost three months of the tour. The weather is disappointing but the cricket outlook fair.

What a change we have seen in England's fortunes since, with no sort of form behind them, they went to Brisbane for the First Test and pulled off a stunning victory. To their success in the Fourth Test, in Melbourne, they have now added four more in a row in the pyjama game bonanzas in Perth, while Australia have lost another three. Allan Border has admitted publicly that his job as captain must be in jeopardy if things don't get better. Since he took over the captaincy, Australia have won just three Test Matches in 25. 'What I want and need,' he says, 'is for our players to perform to their full potential. We just need to win a bloody match again!' Well, cricket is a fickle jade, and who can be certain how the final Test Match, starting here tomorrow, will be resolved?

England's selection problem looks to be a simple one: they will pick 12, adding Phil Edmonds, who did not play in the Challenge final against Pakistan, to the eleven who did. Then, assuming that the recent character of Sydney's pitch has shown no change, they will choose two spinners as they have done all series, preserving a balanced attack, and leave out Gladstone Small or Phillip DeFreitas.

The vote, I think, must now go – if not by much – against DeFreitas. Small has bowled so consistently accurately in recent games, and did so famously when given his chance in the Melbourne Test, that he deserves another here. In that event DeFreitas, a young player of exciting all-round potential, need not despair. He has done so well to play in all the Tests so far. His bowling this past week in Perth has been very lively and straight: a fine display when he knew that his Test place was on the line.

I don't suppose Mike Gatting is aware of the fact, but if England win this Fifth Test match they will achieve their most decisive success in a five-Test series out here since Douglas Jardine's team recovered the Ashes in 1932/33 by a margin of four matches to one.

January 10 (first day, Fifth Test)

They make a satisfactory start towards that objective by taking 7 wickets for 236 after Allan Border wins the toss and chooses to bat first. Australia would be in queer street with-

Peter West reminisces with the great Don Bradman

14 Off-spinner Peter Taylor, a surprise choice for Australia, vindicates his selection with eight wickets in the Fifth Test

15 Dean Jones on his way to an undefeated 184 in the first innings of the Sydney Test

David Gower, elegant as ever, in action during the Fifth Test

Mike Gatting holds aloft the Perth Challenge Trophy

18 Frank Tyson reporting for *The Daily Telegraph* at Adelaide – 'Now how shall I put that in my piece for London?'

19 Mr Justice John Woodcock of *The Times* presiding over a Yuletide press court at which some rather fruity charges were laid...

Peter Smith – 'tour leader' of the press gang – and Geoff Boycott, reporting for the *Daily Mail*

Trevor Bailey, Alec Bedser and Brian Johnston during the Sydney Test

22 Peter West with Ian Botham and another victim of his all-round sporting prowess

Phil Edmonds, David Gower, Henry Blofeld (in foreground), Scyld Berry of
The Observer and Peter West on an epic 26-hour train journey across Australia

Relaxing with Frances and Phil Edmonds

25 Despite the best efforts of Greg Matthews, skipper Mike Gatting leads
England to victory in the World Series Cup Final as (26) Chris Broad takes
another half-century off the Australian attack

out Jones (119 not out) who gets his third international hundred in nine days but his first in a home Test Match and his first against England.

The pitch turns out to be easy paced but offers just enough occasional movement off the seam to whet the quick bowlers' appetites. Dilley is not quite at his best and Botham, at mostly medium pace, looks rather innocuous, but Small bowls right through the morning for the wicket of Marsh and later adds 4 more to achieve the five-card trick yet again. It is another splendid performance but he looks distinctly lucky to pull off one of them. Waugh is given out first ball, caught by a leaping Richards off – as the replay appears to indicate – his forearm. No doubt England think that is something less than adequate compensation for Jones being reprieved on 5 when there is an enormous shout for another catch behind (and the replay suggests it is well justified). Jones may also be fortunate to survive an lbw appeal from Small when he has made three runs more, and he is certainly so, on 41, when he takes a hazardous single to mid-off whence Gower's throw, if it had hit the stumps, would have left him some way from home. However, not too many Test hundreds are made without a bit of luck along the way. This is a fine effort by Jones, a young player instinctively aggressive, endowed with a handsome armoury of strokes, who now reveals continuing restraint and good judgement.

I am still not quite sure how Border manages to swat Edmonds into the hands of Botham, close in round the corner, after making a patient but ominously safe 34. It ends a partnership of 91 with Jones, and Australia, at one time 149 for 2, are subsequently on the slide. Small has an inspired spell of 4 for 22 off 32 deliveries, the last of them off the second new ball which, encouragingly, will be only 6 overs old when England renew operations tomorrow.

Surprised that no requirement has come in from Sportsed for a few paras about the early morning play for later editions back home, I conclude that a check call to the night editor (at midnight GMT) might not come amiss. A lady's voice answers from his desk, and the following conversation ensues:

> P.W.: 'This is Peter West in Sydney. It's just a check call to make sure you don't want anything on the early play here.'
> Lady: 'The early play on what?'
> P.W.: 'On the final Test Match.'
> Lady: 'Oh! Will you hold on. I'll have a word.'

(A two-minute gap ensues.)

> Lady: 'Did you say Test Match? Who's playing who?'
> P.W. (striving to be patient): 'England and Australia.'
> Lady: 'Oh, really. Is it very exciting?'
> P.W.: 'Well, hardly yet. They've just started to bowl the first over.'
> Lady: 'Oh! I think if it's not very spectacular, we don't want anything.'

January 11 (second day, Fifth Test)

Australia 343, England 132 for 5 – with the pitch giving obvious help to Australia's latest bowler, Peter Taylor. *Their* day, for which they have waited a long time, without a doubt, and even the dourest Pom shouldn't begrudge them their relief and pleasure.

In the old days, before one-day cricket attracted a new audience and emphasised different values, would Australia have been barracked when quietly extending their first innings to 343? It takes England another three hours to get the last 3 wickets on an apparently benign pitch. Taylor, who bats left handed, keeps Jones company for another 75 minutes, and Hughes, whose Test batting average is a modest 2.00, sticks around for even longer. Jones carries his bat for 184, and receives the ovation his innings has demanded. He has held the whole piece together for nine hours. It has been a monumental effort by a handsome strokemaker whose natural instinct is to attack.

England may be thinking that if Hughes can bat so comfortably against anything Gatting devises, there is the prospect of another substantial first innings ahead of them. Instant re-think called for. They plunge to 17 for 3, Athey caught off a glove, Gatting lbw to Reid (it looks a very dubious decision), Broad plumb leg before when completely misjudging the line of Hughes. 3 wickets, indeed, for 1 run in 11 balls. Sydneysiders go berserk.

Gower now leads a blazing English counterattack with an array of strokes such as only he can unfurl. Reid goes for four boundaries in one over, the last of them caressed past cover point. Lamb starts hazardously but eagerly joins the chase. In no time at all England's run rate is up to 4 an over and another crowd not far short of 25,000 is being treated to some eventful cricket of all sorts.

Border now gives Taylor his first Test Match bowl. He is a tallish man who at once extracts quite a lot of turn and, what is more, quite a degree of bounce. Lamb aims to cut him in his third over and, given out caught behind, stands there momentarily, as if unable to believe the decision. Enter Botham, who hits the first two balls he receives for off side 4s. In Taylor's next over another disappears into the crowd behind long-on. In the one after that he is caught off bat and pad.

That is not the end of the excitement. But for a coat of varnish, Gower is bowled by Taylor; the ball turns and lifts. The next one, off a wild shot, just clears cover point. And, in the last over, Gower escapes being lbw to Taylor by the proverbial whisker. He looks, as they say, in front of everything. However, he is still there, having stroked no fewer than 11 silken fours in a memorable innings of 62 not out.

There has been an important media hand-out today about a match due to be played on the Test rest day, and known as Clash for the Ash: 'Chris Lander (*Sun*) has been removed from the captaincy of the English Press XI for the match against their Australian counterparts on January 13. The disciplinary committee announced their decision today with "no deep regret or sadness" after Lander had missed a full net practice at the WACA last week. But because of the public humiliation that is bound to follow, the committee have decided to save him from any further financial embarrassment, and no fine will be imposed.'

Lander issued the following statement after hearing of the committee's decision: 'This has come as a real body blow, but I had already told the disciplinary committee that if I was sacked as captain, I would accept that decision and step down. The saddest part of this whole sorry business is that I heard of the decision by car telephone while in the back of a stretch limo (limousine).'

Lander's sacking puts in doubt his $200 a year contract with the Worcester Gazette where his weekly column is ghosted by Ian Botham. The English press selection committee are pleased to hear that Jack Bannister, 76, has answered their SOS in the affirmative and will come out of retirement to lead their XI in his first game since the Bodyline series.

January 12 (third day, Fifth Test)

Australia this evening are 74 for 2 wickets in their second innings, 142 runs ahead, and we have certainly got a fine game of cricket on our hands. Border's side must be scenting victory. I don't think England would fancy having to make 250 or more in the fourth innings on a pitch now slower in pace but with enough in it to have the spinners flexing their fingers. Taylor (Peter Who? when selected) had 6 for 78 when England were bowled out for 275, and is now the latest Australian sporting hero. Edmonds and Emburey turn the screw this evening when confronting Jones and Border in a riveting piece of cricket. All three results remain possible, although the least likely of them has to be another win for England. For that to happen, their bowlers will need to make rapid progress tomorrow.

After yesterday's red-blooded fare, events on this third day, taken all through, are inevitably more mundane. No occasion for heroics by either side. Certainly not by England when Gower departs early on, having a dash at Taylor and being caught at extra cover. The situation demands that those following him get their heads down. Richards (46), Emburey (69) and Small (14) do just that.

Richards plays the spinners especially well. He has looked a different batsman altogether since getting that confident hundred in the Second Test. I describe Emburey for my readers as the Admirable Crichton of this England side: a man tailoring his every action to the needs of the moment. A temporary groin strain impels him to have Athey running for him but does not deter him from taking 14 off one over from Reid. Small, I think, should go in a bit higher. He is a good enough batsman to develop into a versatile Test performer.

When Australia go in a second time, he and Dilley bowl an opening spell in which for some while they enjoy no luck at all. Dilley has found his fire and rhythm again, and eventually he has Marsh beautifully taken at first slip by Emburey, who has taken some exciting catches this tour and never seems to miss anything. Ritchie also fails again, pushing forward to Edmonds and falling to a diving catch by Botham at slip.

Border is 38 not out at the close, having dealt severely with Dilley as he tires a little towards the end of his 10-over stint. He adventures much less against the spinners. Jones is restricted to a mere 6 runs in 80 minutes. Now for the rest day.

There has been a nice touch today from Benson and Hedges, prime sponsors of Australian cricket. They organise what is termed a strictly sexist cruise around Sydney's stunning waterfront for the wives, children and girl friends of players and media. No men allowed. Ambrosia and nectar liberally provided.

January 13 (rest day, Fifth Test)

And no shortage of Bollinger champagne on board the craft conveying England's cricket team to Watson's Bay for a splendid lunch at Doyle's. This is followed by a match on the sands against the Bollinger Belles, enthusiastically captained by Diana Fisher who knows how to bend the laws of the game. England are humiliated.

I understand that towards the end of the party, Henry Blofeld, the only member of the Pommie press to attend it, is thrown into the sea, fully clothed, by Messrs. Broad, DeFreitas, Slack and Small. Henry has a fine sense of humour. On this occasion he needs all of it, having omitted, at the critical moment, to part company with a rather expensive camera.

I last saw Sydney cricket ground in the Australian autumn of 1975, when England played a rugby union international here. Old timers may regret that some of its traditional charm has been lost. The famous Hill, where the barrackers used to hold sway, has been much reduced in size. Yet SCG has been developed into a magnificent arena, the new stands with their variously coloured seating putting me in mind of the Parc des Princes stadium in Paris.

Opinion seems divided about the giant TV screen, a feature both here and in Melbourne. I think it is a splendid addition to amenities already far superior to those on English Test Match grounds. But it ought not to show controversial replays which inflict quite unfair pressure on the wretched umpires. It so happens that both of them, Peter McConnell and Steve Randell, are having a poor game in this final Test.

As I have remarked before, one of the pleasures of working in Australian press boxes is to receive a flow of factual information directly from the official scorers, who on most Test Match grounds are stationed in the same area. Here in Sydney the Australian scorer is Ernie Cosgrove, schoolmaster and cricket statistician. Instantly 'on the ball' with every vital statistic, and conveying it to the scribes through his microphone, he is the nonpareil amongst his trade.

The West Indies, currently playing in Queensland, have been whingeing about the one-day regulation in this country that prohibits short-pitched bowling rising above shoulder height.

'The deliberate removal of the bouncer from one-day cricket,' Viv Richards has been reported as saying, 'robs the traditional batsman–bowler conflict of its necessary potency. It is ridiculous that a bowler is not able to make full use of his abilities. It is like we have all been sent back to play at kindergarten.'

Malcolm Marshall is quoted as saying: 'One-day games are biased too heavily in the batsman's favour to preserve consistent personal motivation. It is very frustrating. You are really at the batsman's mercy because you are unable to retaliate if he has just struck you for 4. The wicket is always dead flat and gives nothing to the bowler.'

Well, it didn't seem like that when West Indies had Australia hopping about in Perth recently. Nor did there seem to be any lack of motivation in a game which followed two rather humbling West Indian defeats in a row.

'I think it is sad,' Viv Richards added, 'but if some of the rules are not changed it will be the end of the game.'

It is a very good rule the Australians have, and I am sure they will not be changing it. Its retention will not mean the end of a game which has become an immensely popular form of entertainment here. So far as the traditional game is concerned, it has been encouraging to learn that English and Australian officials are determined to press a united case within the International Cricket Conference for a further limitation on intimidatory bowling which permits one bouncer – no more than that – in any over.

We see some of them on the evening of this rest day, at a party very generously hosted by Bernie Coleman at the Royal Sydney Golf Club, overlooking Rose Bay. Cocktails served on manicured lawns as lush as any I have seen. Idyllic view over the waterfront. A cloudless sky. And back home, to judge by the latest news, they are enduring the coldest winter for years. How lucky can we get?

News, on return to base, of a sensational victory for English press over Australian press in the Clash for the Ash. The home side have made 127. The Poms need 2 runs to win off the last ball of the match, their last pair at the wicket. Scyld Berry (*Observer*) is the man of the hour with a shrewd inside edge which misses his leg stump and speeds for 4. Christopher Martin-Jenkins is man of the match for the 50 he had made earlier.

I have something of a guilt complex scribbling these thoughts when everyone back home is suffering the big freeze. It is all but removed by John Thicknesse, whose wife, Ann, has rung his sports desk at the *Standard* with a hapless tale of pipes frozen, rooms flooded, no electricity and the Fire Brigade called in to smash holes in the ceiling. Desk rings J.T. and leaves message: 'Please call back. There's a crisis.' Eventually he gets message and returns the call. 'Crisis?' he inquires, panic-stricken. The domestic situation is explained. 'Thank God,' J.T. replies. 'I thought I'd missed a story.' The marriage endures.

January 14 (fourth day, Fifth Test)

Yet another splendidly combative day, at the end of which England, left to make 320 to win off a minimum of 108 overs, have made 39 for 1 wicket, that of Broad, caught and bowled by Sleep. Can they pull off a third victory in the series tomorrow? Every result remains possible, an Australian success the most likely of them, I fancy, if their spinners bowl well and the catches are held.

There can't be any doubt about the behaviour of a pitch on which Taylor got 6 wickets for one side and Emburey has got 7 in a row for the other. His figures of 46-14-78-7 are the best he has returned in Test cricket: a noble effort by a man who has struggled in the field with the groin strain that troubled him two days ago. There is certainly some turn for the spinners, but nothing devilish. Batsmen prepared to sell their lives dearly can endure on it provided they attempt nothing too ambitious. A lot will depend tomorrow on whether England can come through the first session without undue mishap. In these conditions you need a good platform for a longish chase. The previous occasion when England, batting last, made more than 300 to win a Test Match was against Australia in the Third Test in 1928/29, when Percy Chapman's outstanding side scored 332 for 7 wickets. That indicates the size of the present job.

At lunch today England must have been thinking they would have no need to get as many. Nothing much happens in the first half hour, except a flurry of fine strokes from Jones. But from 106 for 2 at one stage Australia subside to 145 for 7 at the interval. Edmonds has Border caught at the wicket, then Emburey gets 4, including Jones, for 10 runs off 49 balls.

No further joy, alas, all through the second session of play, and certainly none as Edmonds lures Waugh out of his crease when he has made 15 and Richards misses a not difficult stumping. How important, in the final analysis, will that be? Waugh makes no further mistake until he gets out for a fine 73. He and the left-handed Taylor add 98 in an absorbing piece of cricket but a very frustrating one for England.

We know what an exciting prospect Waugh can be. He has already played three handsome innings in this series. Taylor's tenure at the crease in this match is extended overall to four hours which, taken in conjunction with his remarkably successful debut as a bowler, must have tempted a man whose feet remain firmly planted on *terra firma* to believe that Test cricket is an absolute doddle. One match for New South Wales this season, and Grade stuff for the rest of it!

Gatting has briefly to give a new ball to Small and Botham, the last named to have his final bowl for England in an overseas Test Match, in order that his spinners can use something that may bounce a bit higher. Nothing much happens for some while, but at length Waugh makes his second mistake, holing out off Emburey to Athey at long on, and a lame vice-captain is soon taking his bow as he leads his side from the field.

Botham has had three final overs only because of the early departure today of Dilley, who throws his arm out when returning a ball from long leg. This, we hear, may entail him missing the first of England's games in the one-day World Series Cup which will occupy the rest of the tour. We already have two men in the side, Gower and Athey, who have persistent 'arm' problems. Gatting has been able to disguise them pretty well overall, though it has sometimes required him to field further away from the wicket than a captain ideally likes to be.

Back for a moment, amidst all this exciting cricket, to another local plus. The sightscreens at SCG are electronically controlled, rolling smoothly one way or t'other at the touch of a button. Why can't we devise something similar in England?

January 15 (fifth day, Fifth Test)

Australia by 55 runs, with just one over to spare. It has been, to use one of Mike Gatting's favourite adjectives, a tremendous day – a thrilling finale to what, quite simply, has been one of the most gripping Test Matches I have ever watched. We are of course sorry to lose it, but it is better to have a positive result rather than the anticlimax of a draw and, heaven knows, Australia, 14 previous Tests without a win, have been in desperate need of a heady draught.

To pull off victory themselves, and thus make it 3–0 in the series with 2 drawn, England need a solid platform for later exploitation. This they get as Athey and Gower push the score along to 91 for 1. Alas, some nasty hiccoughs either side of lunch. Gower is caught off Border at short leg – the Australian skipper's first Test wicket in almost four years; Athey tries an injudicious sweep against Sleep and is bowled behind his legs. Now, at the interval, it is 91 for 3. But worse follows. Lamb is caught off Taylor via bat and pad almost at once, and Botham departs first ball, to a fine, diving, one-handed catch by Wellham at midwicket. 102 for 5: England back on their heels, retrenchment called for and the target of 320 seeming a long way distant.

We now witness from John Bull Gatting a remarkably forceful performance. As I think I have written before, the England captain has no great opinion of spin bowling, but he now has to contend with it on a helpful pitch. It is one thing to 'prop and cop', quite another to make rapid headway. Yet Gatting, with Richards a most able, confident ally, carries the fight through the rest of the afternoon session and beyond the tea interval to a point where, the last 20 mandatory overs now due, England need another 90 for victory. Four and a half runs an over, 5 wickets in hand. 'I thought,' Border says afterwards, 'that we'd then had it.'

But in the second of those overs Gatting is caught and bowled by Waugh, denied by 4 runs what would have been a marvellous hundred. It is a very different picture now. Emburey has been told by his captain to 'get in' and then take things as they come. But it is soon apparent that the drawbridge has been raised, England now fighting for survival, Australia ringing the bat. The atmosphere is supercharged, on and off the field.

Runs are of no consequence now, only time and wickets. Richards, who has done a splendid job, and Emburey, as cool and as experienced as they come, take England 9 overs nearer to safe haven. Then Sleep twists the tale again. With one ball he has Richards playing on to his occasional wrong 'un off the inside edge. With the next, he has Edmonds pushing forward, playing no stroke, and lbw. 2 wickets left, 9 overs remaining.

Seven of these, Small having thwarted Sleep's hat-trick, are safely negotiated. But for the 18th over Border turns back to Reid, and with his fourth ball he has Small edging it to first slip, where Border accepts a difficult, tumbling catch only inches from the ground. Enter the last man, Dilley. 14 balls to go.

He takes 2 off the first, keeps the next one out. The penultimate over is bowled by Sleep, although Border admits afterwards that it was touch and go whether he brought back Hughes. Emburey blocks out the first 5 but the last one, a leg-break, keeps low and the vice-captain, on his back foot, is bowled to a whoop of Australian joy. Sleep has taken 5 for 72 but it is Taylor who is named as man of the match. Not a bad way to begin a Test career? Chris Broad is man of the series, and quite right, too, after those three hundreds in successive Tests. He wins himself four handsome goblets and a gold tray. 'Shall we melt them down for the team kitty?' Gatting enquires. And then he adds: 'I don't like losing, but good luck to Allan Border. I know how he has felt on a losing run. It's been a great game of cricket. It could have gone either way.' Indeed it could. Those of us privileged to watch it all won't soon forget.

January 16

To Brisbane, for the start tomorrow of the World Series Cup. The city steams in a sauna bath temperature. Bowlers will hope for something less enervating when we play West Indies.

I file some thoughts on the Test series, suggesting that England need feel no shame after losing a match such as this, and certainly not after losing the toss and batting last. I reflect that while Australia rejoice to have won again, England have brought their own calendar year to an encouraging close. I think Mike Gatting has had a fine tour both as batsman and captain. He has made five good scores in the Tests, deserving to have a second hundred, in Sydney, to add to the one he got in Adelaide.

FIFTH TEST

Sydney, 10–15 January 1987

AUSTRALIA

	1st innings		2nd innings	
G. R. Marsh	c Gatting b Small	24	c Emburey b Dilley	14
G. M. Ritchie	lbw b Dilley	6	c Botham b Edmonds	13
D. M. Jones	not out	184	c Richards b Emburey	30
A. R. Border*	c Botham b Edmonds	34	b Edmonds	49
D. M. Wellham	c Richards b Small	17	c Lamb b Emburey	1
S. R. Waugh	c Richards b Small	0	c Athey b Emburey	73
P. R. Sleep	c Richards b Small	9	c Lamb b Emburey	10
T. J. Zoehrer†	c Gatting b Small	12	lbw b Emburey	1
P. L. Taylor	c Emburey b Edmonds	11	c Lamb b Emburey	42
M. G. Hughes	c Botham b Edmonds	16	b Emburey	5
B. A. Reid	b Dilley	4	not out	1
Extras	(b 12, lb 4, w 2, nb 8)	26	(b 5, lb 7)	12
TOTAL		343		251

Fall of wickets: 8, 58, 149, 184, 184, 200, 232, 271, 338.
Second innings: 29, 31, 106, 110, 115, 141, 145.

Bowling: Dilley 23.5-5-67-2; Small 33-11-75-5; Botham 23-10-42-0; Emburey 30-4-62-0; Edmonds 34-5-79-3; Gatting 1-0-2-0.
Second innings: Dilley 15-4-48-1; Small 8-2-17-0; Edmonds 43-16-79-2; Emburey 46-15-78-7; Botham 3-0-17-0; Gatting 2-2-0-0.

ENGLAND

	1st innings		2nd innings	
B. C. Broad	lbw b Hughes	6	c&b Sleep	17
C. W. J. Athey	c Zoehrer b Hughes	5	b Sleep	31
M. W. Gatting*	lbw b Reid	0	c&b Waugh	96
A. J. Lamb	c Zoehrer b Taylor	24	c Waugh b Taylor	3
D. I. Gower	c Wellham b Taylor	72	c Marsh b Border	37
I. T. Botham	c Marsh b Taylor	16	c Wellham b Taylor	0
C. J. Richards†	c Wellham b Reid	46	b Sleep	38
J. E. Emburey	b Taylor	69	b Sleep	22
P. H. Edmonds	c Marsh b Taylor	3	lbw b Sleep	0
G. C. Small	b Taylor	14	c Border b Reid	0
G. R. Dilley	not out	4	not out	2
Extras	(b 9, lb 3, w 2, nb 2)	16	(b 8, lb 6, w 1, nb 3)	18
TOTAL		275		264

Fall of wickets: 16, 17, 17, 89, 119, 142, 213, 219, 270..
Second innings: 24, 91, 91, 102, 102, 233, 257, 257, 262.

Bowling: Hughes 16-3-58-2; Reid 25-7-74-2; Waugh 6-4-6-0; Taylor 26-7-78-6; Sleep 21-6-47-0.
Second innings: Hughes 12-3-32-0; Reid 19-8-32-1; Taylor 29-10-76-2; Sleep 35-14-72-5; Border 13-6-25-1; Waugh 6-2-13-1.

Toss: Australia.
Umpires: P. J. McConnell and S. G. Randell.

As a captain out in the field, he has defended shrewdly when it has been necessary but revealed an always positive attitude at other times. He has been well liked by everybody, including Australians. I hope he now feels happier about the captaincy overall; he certainly should do. But in the unlikely event of him stepping down, I would without any hesitation name John Emburey as his successor. He is an admirably composed and versatile cricketer, with a shrewd mind. Groin strain notwithstanding, he bowled for some 15 hours in the Sydney Test and batted for almost five. He has been the top wicket taker with 18. Edmonds has got 15. What a pleasure to see two England spinners playing throughout the series.

I wish Ian Botham could have brought his overseas Test career to a more exciting end. No wickets, 16 in the first innings, 0 first ball in the second. He has been so immensely determined to finish on a high. Yet the fact is that apart from his brilliant hundred in Brisbane, five wickets in Melbourne when in overdrive, and some good catches, he has not made the impact on the series he hoped for. Yet that hundred at the Gabba, following Athey's priceless batting throughout the critical first day there – and all this after England had some harrowing form behind them, and despaired of getting a proper start to their innings – contributed crucially to an astonishing victory. It simply stunned Australia. In the Second Test, after another huge score, England had the initiative but their bowlers were frustrated by a pitch which belied its ominous appearance. In the Third, without Botham, England did well to mount a holding operation with only four front line bowlers. In the Fourth, Broad made his third hundred in successive Tests, Botham came up trumps as a bowler – as did Gladstone Small, in Graham Dilley's absence – the series was won and retention of the Ashes assured.

Broad has had a great tour: almost 500 Test runs at an average of 69. Athey, with 96 in Perth, certainly proved the answer as a stopgap opener. I think that England next summer should open with Broad and Graham Gooch, and drop Athey down to his right place at No. 3. They need someone there to drop anchor if need be. Gower, Lamb, Gatting and Botham are natural aggressors.

I fear for Lamb's Test place. In this series he has averaged only 18; he has made only three 50s in his last 39 Test innings. Yet he has always looked in good touch on this tour. Too confident, perhaps; in a little bit too much of a hurry. For all his troubles earlier, David Gower has still topped 400 Test runs and no one, but no one, has made the game look such a very simple and elegant matter.

There is no doubt in my mind that Bruce French has been the better of the two wicketkeepers out here. But the England selectors wanted the bonus of Jack Richards's batting, and he provided a very confident answer with a splendid hundred in the Second Test and more useful innings later. Phillip DeFreitas, Phil Edmonds and Gladstone Small have all contributed some useful runs – in addition of course to Emburey amongst the lower order.

Graham Dilley on this tour has proved himself as a consistently hostile strike bowler, highly respected. Small, so regularly accurate, grabbed two chances with telling effect. DeFreitas made 40 at Brisbane, as well as taking five wickets in the match, but later, on unhelpful pitches, found them much harder to get. He remains a very exciting prospect. We rave about his lithe fielding and his thrilling arm. And, writing about fielding, it's worth a note that England mostly held their catches while Australia, at least until the final Test, did not.

It is inevitable on tour that some players miss out. James Whitaker, Neil Foster, Bruce French and Wilf Slack . . . they have been the unlucky ones, sitting patiently and cheerfully in the wings. I think England should give them a spin in a few of the remaining one-day bonanzas.

January 17 (World Series Cup preliminary v. West Indies)

England are involved in the first of eight preliminary games they will play here, there and seemingly everywhere for the Benson and Hedges World Series Cup, and I must say it's not every day of the week that they beat West Indies, whether it's the one-day or the longer game. My word, by 6 wickets in a canter, and but for Gower and Lamb 'giving it away', as they say, it could have been by more.

It has been a very good toss for Gatting to win. West Indies are put in and then bowled out for 154. The ball swings in debilitating heat, well into the 90s. It cuts off the seam. Dilley, DeFreitas and Small use it splendidly. Greenidge and Richards both go for 0. From 26 for 3 Haynes and Logie mount a recovery but both get themselves out assaulting Emburey, and no major batsman is left to plunder the last 10 overs. England make sure that no one else does, Dilley roaring back with 2 more wickets at the end of the innings.

Play having started at 10 a.m., England begin their reply at 2.15 p.m. and it is all over before 5. The pitch now plays more easily, and they never looked under the slightest pressure. Broad and Athey provide a useful base, Broad, after a subdued start, makes a flowing 49, and Gower thrills everybody, save perhaps Holding, with some glorious strokes on the off side. He has reached 42 off the same number of balls when he perpetrates an inelegant hoick to mid on. When Lamb departs to a catch at long on, Botham arrives to be dropped by Holding in the deep field and then to smash the winning blow.

West Indies have now lost four out of their last five one-day internationals. England here have now succeeded in five in a row. It looks today as if the West Indies captain decided quite early in the England innings that he cannot win. When Harper bowls his off spin, England need less than 80 with 8 wickets in hand. Yet Richards sets the field defensively back. He bowls 10 overs himself. Dilley got the

BENSON AND HEDGES
WORLD SERIES CUP PRELIMINARY

17 January 1987

WEST INDIES

C. G. Greenidge	lbw b DeFreitas	0
D. L. Haynes	c DeFreitas b Emburey	43
R. B. Richardson	c Botham b Dilley	15
I. V. A. Richards	b Dilley	0
A. L. Logie	c Lamb b Emburey	46
P. J. L. Dujon	b DeFreitas	22
R. A. Harper	lbw b Small	2
M. D. Marshall	b Dilley	13
M. A. Holding	c Richards b Emburey	0
J. Garner	c Richards b Dilley	1
C. A. Walsh	not out	5
Extras	(lb 4)	4
TOTAL (46.3 overs)		154

Fall of wickets: 1, 26, 26, 112, 120, 122, 174, 148, 151.

Bowling: Dilley 8.3-1-23-4; DeFreitas 9-2-17-2; Botham 10-1-46-0; Small 10-1-29-1; Emburey 9-0-33-3.

ENGLAND

B. C. Broad	b Richards	49
C. W. J. Athey	c Dujon b Holding	14
D. I. Gower	c Garner b Harper	42
A. J. Lamb	c sub (W. K. Benjamin) b Harper	22
M. W. Gatting*	not out	3
I. T. Botham	not out	14
Extras	(lb 2, w 2, nb 8)	12
TOTAL (4 wkts: 43.1 overs)		156

Did not bat: C. J. Richards, P. A. J. DeFreitas, J. E. Emburey, G. R. Dilley, G. C. Small.

Fall of wickets: 30, 91, 134, 140.

Bowling: Marshall 5-1-11-0; Garner 4-0-17-0; Holding 6-0-33-1; Walsh 7.1-0-19-0; Harper 10-0-43-2; Richards 10-0-27-1; Richardson 1-0-4-0.

man of the match award against West Indies in Perth. He now receives another. There ought to be a special medal for Small who is so dehydrated after bowling 6 excellent overs that he has to come off for ice packs and the intake of several pints of liquid. Later, he sends down another imposing spell.

January 18 (World Series Cup preliminary v. Australia)

It would be nice to reflect that England have got away with two good wins in the World Series Cup, but they miss out against Australia today by 11 runs. It has been a very tough assignment, playing on consecutive days in sweltering heat, and some of today's performance looks jaded. None the less, England should have won after Australia had left them to make 262 on a very flat and easy paced pitch.

Gower, Lamb and Botham all get themselves out to needlessly ambitious strokes, and a weary Athey, having held the piece together after an airy start, gets bogged down as his hundred approaches when he ought to be throwing the bat. Athey shares with another Yorkshireman, Boycott, a reluctance, even an inability, to depart from refined methods.

Gatting supplies some rugged ones, making 30 off 25 balls. Richards and DeFreitas perish in a good cause. But Emburey and Small are left to get 34 off the last 2 overs, which asks a great deal. Even so, Emburey has a good dart at it with three flashing 4s in the penultimate over and another in the last.

I must not forget to add that Gower blots his escutcheon by knocking all three stumps askew with his bat after being bowled by Waugh. Peter Lush says later that it was purely a gesture of frustration and disappointment with himself, and he intends no official action. It was also a totally uncharacteristic one for someone always thought to be laid back and relaxed.

The Australian No. 3, Dean Jones, is finding it a blissfully easy game this month. He had two one-day hundreds in Perth. Now he gets a third – not to mention his 184 in the final Test Match. He and Marsh put on 178 for the second wicket after Australia have won the toss, and Jones in due course wins the man of the match award. England's bowlers stick it out well.

We now need West Indies to beat Australia in Sydney later this week to level things off in the prelims. Meantime, England's players are given the next three days off. It has been a long, hard tour and they have certainly earned them.

It has occurred to me that I have now been working every day in Australia for more than three months, and Sportsed has not yet brought himself to suggest that I might have one off. So I decide to give myself one tomorrow, and indicate as much on Tandy. In common, I think, with all my collea-gues, I am finding it a hard, demanding tour, although I dare say all my cricketing friends believe the life of a reporter to be purely hedonistic. This is a reflection, not a complaint. I'm very lucky to be here.

January 19

Graham is still, it seems, Dilley-dallying about re-signing for Kent, in spite of the recent presence in Sydney of his county captain, Chris Cowdrey, who, one assumes, has been urging him to put pen to paper. It now appears that Ian Botham was not the only England cricketer on Duncan Fearnley's shopping list when the Worces-tershire chairman flew out for the Fifth Test. Graham Otway, who is writing a book for Dilley, has broken news of a probable Dilley/Worcestershire agreement in *Today* back home.

The Somerset-based company, Car Phone, which is putting up enough cash for Worcestershire to sign Botham, must now have earmarked a lot more to persuade Dilley to sacrifice his eventual Benefit year with Kent. Professional

BENSON AND HEDGES
WORLD SERIES CUP PRELIMINARY

18 January 1987

AUSTRALIA

G. R. Marsh	lbw b Dilley	93
D. M. Wellham	c Emburey b Small	26
D. M. Jones	b Emburey	101
A. R. Border	b Dilley	11
S. R. Waugh	not out	14
S. P. O'Donnell	not out	3
Extras	(lb 9, w 3, nb 1)	13
TOTAL (for 4 wkts, 50 overs)		261

Did not bat: G. R. J. Matthews, K. H. Macleay, T. J. Zoehrer, P. L. Taylor; B. A. Reid.

Fall of wickets: 48, 226, 234, 246.

Bowling: Dilley 10-2-40-2; DeFreitas 10-2-41-0; Small 10-0-57-1; Botham 10-0-54-0; Emburey 10-0-60-1.

ENGLAND

B. C. Broad	c Matthews b O'Donnell	15
C. W. J. Athey	c O'Donnell b Reid	111
D. I. Gower	b Waugh	15
A. J. Lamb	c Marsh b Matthews	6
I. T. Botham	b O'Donnell	22
M. W. Gatting*	b Taylor	30
C. J. Richards†	c O'Donnell b Reid	7
P. A. J. DeFreitas	c Border b Waugh	6
J. E. Emburey	not out	24
G. C. Small	run out	2
G. R. Dilley	not out	0
Extras	(b 1, lb 10, nb 1)	12
TOTAL (for 9 wkts, 50 overs)		250

Fall of wickets: 48, 73, 92, 148, 192, 210, 218, 225, 250.

Bowling: Macleay 8-0-39-0; Reid 10-1-34-2; O'Donnell 10-0-59-2; Waugh 9-0-56-2; Matthews 10-0-34-1; Taylor 3-0-17-1.

cricketers can't be blamed for gathering rosebuds while they may, but English cricket seems to be edging closer to a transfer system, which the TCCB, working with the Cricketers' Association, will need to guard against. There should still be something to be said for old loyalties.

Anyway, Duncan Fearnley has moved on to New Zealand, ostensibly in order to persuade the all-rounder, Dipak Patel, to change his mind about seeking a Test career there, and Alan Hurd, Botham's solicitor, is flying back to London with a reported new client, Dilley, on his books.

Sportsed sends me a telex, a civil one, asking me to keep him posted about Dilley/Worcestershire. I tell him I will keep my ears to the ground at this end, but suggest the next chapter may unfold at his end, after the Kent committee have met to discuss the matter further, and perhaps to increase their offer. Meanwhile, Dilley is dropping his wrist here. 'Nothing has yet been decided,' he asserts.

January 20

Sixty thousand spectators watch West Indies beat Australia in the third World Series Cup preliminary in Melbourne by 7 wickets, which is just the result England wanted. All three countries have now won and lost a game. I view the affair on television from a room at the Chateau Commodore in Sydney which has an uplifting view of the waterfront. I wish I could say that the rest of the services provided by this friendly hotel reached the same lofty standards.

Hearts bleed for Australia, put in to bat on a hard pitch, as their batsmen are chained by the relentless speed and accuracy of the early West Indian bowling. Holding delivers a marvellously restrictive spell: 10 overs for 15 runs. Border gutsily hangs in, and with O'Donnell hoists his side from a hopeless 74 for 5 to a respectable but still inadequate 181 for 6. O'Donnell strikes a brave 52 off 64 balls. Border ends with 64 not out, having, as it happens, contributed only 14 runs in the last 60.

West Indies cruise home, pacing it nicely. Haynes (67, and man of the match) and Logie, 44 not out, ensure victory with a third wicket stand of 79. No need for the injured Viv Richards to bat.

January 21

You can watch all the big cricket on Channel 9 television in Australia provided you don't live in the State where the match is being played. At a Test Match, say, in Sydney, New South Wales viewers get the third session of play on their screens. At a one-day contest they receive the first two hours, by way of appetiser to encourage those close enough to the ground to get along for the game's climax.

The sheer technical brilliance of Channel 9's coverage has to be admired. Not so long ago I used to think they had so many different angled replays to reveal that they over-played their hand, not always finding the right one first. But yesterday, after Dirk Wellham had been run out in a rather unusual fashion, the various replays, step by step, gave the most telling analysis of how it came about.

The coverage, mind you, ought to be pretty good. Channel 9 have 11 cameras at a big game (as compared with the BBC's seven or eight), and all of them are manned by the same experts throughout the summer here. It is only in the last summer or two back home that the BBC's senior cricket producer, Nick Hunter, who has recently been appointed Assistant Head of Outside Broadcasts, has had four regular cameramen on the job.

I suppose the time may be coming when the BBC, like Channel 9, will cover the game from both ends, in other words show it always with the bowler running away from the camera. I am old-fashioned enough to hope it never will, but I have to admit that most of my friends hardly seem to notice the difference. I think it is disorientating not to know which end is which.

Viewers in the UK at least are spared the commercials

which are fired into the system here at the end of every over, when every wicket falls, at the slightest hint of any stoppage for whatever reason and, not infrequently, run across the bottom of the screen as a distraction when the game is actually in progress.

Being unable to talk to their public during commercial breaks, the commentators certainly make up for lost time when they get back into business. They hardly ever stop nattering, but then I have to admit that Australians like a lot of chat and a brasher style of presentation.

Those back home who consider the BBC wastes its money on too many commentators ('who will shortly out-number the antagonists themselves', wrote one enraged Lt Col Ret'd from Dorset) should do a count here. Channel 9 had six former Test players working at yesterday's game in Melbourne, eight, including Bob Willis, at the final Test Match. They work in pairs, chatting away turn and turn about, whereas in England one man would do the basic running commentary and there would be interpolations from the other. In this respect the BBC output is better disciplined. Indeed its whole coverage is more restful. That at least is how I see it, as one who has had a declared interest. With its limited yet increasing resources the BBC's coverage in recent summers has, I think, left very little to be desired. I am also biased in its favour because I like to see the game covered, except for the occasional reverse angle replay, from one end.

Richie Benaud presents the cricket here in his profes-sional, quite unflappable manner, but looks less relaxed than he does in vision in our own country. The forthright Ian Chappell is always worth listening to, and Tony Greig conducts his pre-match 'pitch clinic', including all that stuff about 'players' comfort', with panache. I notice that when they talk to somebody in front of camera, they rarely angle themselves to ensure that viewers get virtually a 'full frontal' of the interviewee. The BBC would never stand for that.

January 22 (World Series Cup preliminary v. Australia)

A night to remember as England, thanks to Allan Lamb, pull off a thrilling victory over Australia by 3 wickets with 1 ball to spare – all this under the floodlights in front of a huge crowd of more than 36,000. A spectacular sight and a quite spectacular and unexpected climax.

When Australia, opting to bat first, are contained to 233 for 8 on an extremely flat pitch, I reckon that England have no business to lose. Nor again when Broad launches their reply by racing to 46 out of 51 with a stream of gracious strokes. Nor yet again after Broad, in end-of-term mood, gives it away, and a steadfast Gower/Lamb partnership keeps their side on course. But Gower (a polished 50), Gatting, Botham, Emburey and Richards all come and go, and England – DeFreitas now joined with Lamb – need 25 off the last 2 overs. The penultimate one, from Waugh, yields only 7. So now, six balls left and Reid to bowl, the requirement is 18. 'I'm afraid it's not on,' I mutter to John Woodcock in the press box. He takes a similarly pessimistic view. But this game of cricket is eternally surprising us, and Lamb ensures that it does so now.

He scampers 2 off the first ball, heaves the second to the square leg boundary and blasts the third for a huge six over midwicket. It's a very different picture now: only 6 wanted off three balls. Lamb hits the next one into the covers and, thanks to a wild overthrow, gets two for a stroke worth only one. So, crucially, he is back at the striking end. Four off two balls. One is enough. Lamb with enormous aplomb clatters it to the square leg boundary again. There is one remarkable statistic about his *coup de main*: he has made 77 off 102 balls, 99 of which he faced before hitting his first 4. No doubt whatsoever about who is man of the match, although I suppose if Australia had won it would have gone to Wellham, for his 97.

Australia in fact have made a mess of their final run-in. A score of 190 for 3 suggested a total round about the 275 mark. But Border is dismissed cheaply and his side muster just 43 off the last 10 overs. All credit, though, to England's outcricket, and the shrewd way in which Gatting handles it. Athey takes three good catches. Altogether, a very timely win which puts England on top of the preliminary table (though West Indies have a game in hand). There were signs in Brisbane last weekend that England were a little jaded, not just by the heat but by the demands of a long tour. This success should get the adrenalin pumping again.

January 23

As we fly back to Adelaide for two more games in the World Series Cup, I reflect for the paper that some also serve who only stand and wait. Bruce French, who lost his Test place to Jack Richards, and then picked up a chest virus, played his last game, against Victoria, in the first half of December. The last match for James Whitaker and Wilf Slack was the Tasmanian one, in Hobart, which finished five weeks ago. That was also Neil Foster's last first-class game, although he managed to get in four overs in Perth on January 5 before leaving the field with a knee injury. That was in a preliminary one-day affair in the Challenge when the two sides involved, England and Pakistan, had already qualified for the final. The better England do in the World Series Cup the more likely they are to stick to a successful combination. I ask Micky Stewart for his thoughts on the four unlucky players. 'They've been as keen as those who've played regularly, and they've done everything possible to contribute to the success of the tour.' I certainly endorse those comments.

It is now taken as virtually read out here that Stewart will become an England selector next season. His presence will bring to their deliberations the views of a man totally familiar with everything that has happened on this tour. That will remedy a long-standing weakness. Stewart has

BENSON AND HEDGES
WORLD SERIES CUP PRELIMINARY

22 January 1987

AUSTRALIA

G. R. Marsh	c Richards b Edmonds	47
D. M. Wellham	c Athey b Emburey	97
D. M. Jones	c Athey b DeFreitas	34
A. R. Border	c Dilley b Edmonds	13
S. R. Waugh	c Athey b Dilley	10
G. R. J. Matthews	c DeFreitas b Emburey	2
K. H. Macleay	b Dilley	12
T. J. Zoehrer	not out	9
P. J. Taylor	st Richards b Emburey	0
Extras	(b 2, lb 5, nb 2)	9
TOTAL (for 8 wkts, 50 overs)		233

Did not bat: S. O'Donnell, B. A. Reid.

Fall of wickets: 109, 156, 189, 205, 208, 208, 230, 233.

Bowling: Dilley 9-2-28-2; DeFreitas 10-0-46-1; Gatting 2-0-11-0; Botham 10-0-51-0; Emburey 9-0-42-3; Edmonds 10-0-48-2.

ENGLAND

B. C. Broad	c Matthews b Taylor	45
C. W. J. Athey	c Zoehrer b Reid	2
D. I. Gower	c Wellham b O'Donnell	50
A. J. Lamb	not out	77
M. W. Gatting*	b O'Connell	1
I. T. Botham	b Waugh	27
J. E. Emburey	run out	4
C. J. Richards†	c Waugh b O'Donnell	3
P. A. J. DeFreitas	not out	6
Extras	(lb 16, nb 1, w 2)	19
TOTAL (for 7 wkts, 48.5 overs)		234

Did not bat: P. H. Edmonds, G. R. Dilley.

Fall of wickets: 33, 51, 137, 143, 186, 191, 202.

Bowling: Mcleay 4-0-22-0; Reid 9.5-3-44-1; Taylor 10-0-42-1; Waugh 5-0-22-1; Matthews 10-1-36-0; Border 3-0-13-0; O'Donnell 6-0-39-3.

144

contributed a great deal to the tactical and technical thinking on this trip, not to mention overall morale. He has a good rapport with the captain and players. He ought now to be asked to manage the England side in the next Cornhill series, against Pakistan, and be offered the job for a minimum of three years.

January 24 (World Series Cup preliminary v. West Indies)

I certainly didn't suppose when I came out here that I would be reporting a third consecutive England victory over West Indies in the one-day game. On this occasion, having made 252 for 6, they bowl out their vaunted opponents for 163, the losing side then remaining incommunicado for an hour and a half in their dressing room for what must have been an interesting post-mortem.

The thermometer pops up to 97 degrees while Broad (55) and Athey (64) provide an ideal platform with 121 for the first wicket at not much less than 4 an over. Even Garner feels the heat. Gower, Botham and Gatting all depart in rapid succession to a variety of adventurous strokes but Lamb (33 not out) keeps the pot simmering, Richards and Emburey make handy contributions and England get 75 off the last 10.

It is a typical Adelaide pitch, and no one takes anything for granted. But things look a lot more promising when DeFreitas, sharing an excellent opening burst with Dilley, swiftly accounts for Greenidge and Richardson, the last named to the one ball all day that did something unpredictable. And even better when Richards, having made an ominously dangerous 43, strikes Botham high to the distant River Torrens end and Broad, running a long way, holds a really testing catch.

This exciting effort by Broad is the turning point and another factor in his man of the match award. West Indian middle batting is not what it used to be; they gradually fall behind the clock, and Emburey chisels his way through the tail enders. Peter Shilton would have admired the catch by Gower that accounts for Logie. Dilley takes two nice ones in the deep field and DeFreitas clings on to one at deep square, narrowly avoiding collision with an equally acquisitive Lamb.

That last catch comes from a bouncer bowled by Emburey. 'Big Joel won't be playing for Somerset next summer,' the vice-captain reflects later. 'I thought I'd let him have one.' It would have been called a no-ball if directed, say, at the diminutive Logie.

January 25

Almost 24,000 spectators cram Adelaide's elegant Oval today to see Australia go down bravely by 16 runs to the West Indies. If they lose to England here tomorrow they will then have to win their last three preliminaries to have a hope of reaching the final stages. It is probably all very confusing to readers back home. I am sure they care, provided England are winning. But how much of this one-day stuff will be remembered in years ahead? I shan't soon forget this recent Test series. The details of what happened in the so-called Challenge in Perth are already blurred.

West Indies, put in first on a grey morning, make a more than adequate 237 for 5 (Richardson 72, Richards 79) but appear to let Australia off the hook when adding only a modest 59 off their last 10 overs. Matthews, 1 for 34 off 10, is respectfully treated but Taylor is not. Why Australia risk two off spinners on a ground with short square boundaries is a mystery. There can be no two thoughts about the length of the straight ones here. Harper carries that at the river Torrens end with one of the biggest hits I have ever seen. About 120 yards hit to pitch. Off Reid.

Marsh gets a valiant 94 for Australia, Jones a forthright 40, but Border goes for a single and, after the departure of Waugh, Australia run out of time and wickets. Not the easiest job in the world to get 79 off the last 10 overs against

BENSON AND HEDGES
WORLD SERIES CUP PRELIMINARY

24 January 1987

ENGLAND

B. C. Broad	st Dujon b Richards	55
C. W. J. Athey	c Marshall b Harper	64
D. I. Gower	c Haynes b Gray	29
I. T. Botham	c Logie b Walsh	7
A. J. Lamb	not out	33
M. W. Gatting	c Dujon b Walsh	3
C. J. Richards	b Marshall	18
J. E. Emburey	not out	16
Extras	(b 4, lb 13, w 5, nb 5)	27
TOTAL (for 6 wkts, 50 overs)		252

Did not bat: P. A. J. DeFreitas, G. C. Small, G. R. Dilley.

Fall of wickets: 121, 148, 161, 177, 182, 220.

Bowling: Marshall 9-1-39-1; Gray 10-0-43-1; Garner 9-1-31-0; Walsh 10-0-55-2; Harper 9-0-46-1; Richards 3-0-21-1.

WEST INDIES

C. G. Greenidge	lbw b DeFreitas	3
D. L. Haynes	b Small	22
R. B. Richardson	c Lamb b DeFreitas	3
I. V. A. Richards	c Broad b Botham	43
A. L. Logie	c Gower b Dilley	43
P. I. Dujon	c Dilley b Emburey	25
R. A. Harper	c Dilley b Emburey	4
M. D. Marshall	c Athey b Emburey	3
J. Garner	c DeFreitas b Emburey	0
A. H. Gray	not out	7
C. A. Walsh	b DeFreitas	3
Extras	(w 2, nb 5)	7
TOTAL (45.5 overs)		163

Fall of wickets: 3, 15, 60, 92, 136, 141, 150, 150, 157.

Bowling: Dilley 8-1-19-1; DeFreitas 7.5-1-15-3; Botham 10-0-46-1; Small 10-1-46-1; Emburey 10-0-37-4.

Marshall and co. Zoehrer is the sort of batsman to cut a dash, but he comes in too late to give Marsh the help he needs.

There has been another Botham story in one of the Sunday papers here. England's champion, it is claimed, has been stopped by England's management from flying by helicopter to a speaking engagement somewhere in South Australia in three days' time. However, it transpires that Messrs. Lush and Stewart know nothing whatever about alleged trip. No one sought official clearance. Another example, no doubt, of some 'fly' up-country agent pulling a fast one without clearing his lines of communication, not just with England's admin. but with Botham's personal manager here, Tom Byron. Botham, I understand, has now parted company with yet another agent in England. Byron will handle his affairs back home as well. That's very good news for Ian, in my book. Tom strikes me as being a sturdy, straight-dealing character. I.B. needs strong management. I hope the alliance works and endures.

January 26 (World Series Cup preliminary v. Australia)

Not a good day at all, the worst cricketing one since England were beaten by New South Wales more than two months back. Thanks to some indisciplined not to say frivolous batting, they throw away the chance of victory over Australia after doing what seems to be the essential groundwork. Australia 225 for 6, England 192 all out – after being at one point 125 for 2.

Some bounce and movement give Dilley and DeFreitas a chance to put Australia's early batsmen on the rack. DeFreitas has Marsh, Wellham and Jones (who could scarcely lay a bat on Dilley) for 10 runs. There is yet another brilliant catch by Emburey, this time at backward point. Border and Waugh now more than tilt the balance with a record tournament stand of 164, Australia's skipper being dropped by Dilley (with the sun in his eyes) off Botham on

29. Australia then miss the boat over the last 10 overs, which yield a modest 66. We contemplate a comfortable England win, eight points from five games and virtual assurance of a place in the final.

Athey does not last long, nor Gower, who plays with much ease and mastery before a flippant hook is excitingly caught by Waugh. We can just about forgive Gower another feckless shot on this tour after Broad and Gatting have produced 70, which puts England well on terms with the clock. Alas and alack, Broad now sells his wicket cheaply, too. Gatting, who looks in rampant order, can't wait to get after Taylor who bowls him with his first ball. Lamb is run out when sent back by Botham (it looks to be Lamb's call). Richards heaves all round a slower full toss. Four gone for 27, things falling apart, 74 wanted off the last 10.

This would be no great problem were Botham in good nick, but it has to be remarked that his batting for some while has been out of sorts (he has also tweaked something in his throwing arm when fielding). It takes him 10 overs to struggle to 18. Then he is stumped off Taylor. A requirement of 52 off the last 5 overs is a lot more than the rest of the batsmen can manage against some tight and fervent Australian outcricket inspired by a crowd of more than 24,000.

It has been Australia Day, in more ways than one. This reprieve keeps their cricket team in the hunt. There will surely be an enormous host to witness their game against West Indies in Sydney in two days' time.

No excuses from England's skipper, who ruefully reflects that the batting has let them down three times against Australia in this tournament (Lamb got them out of trouble in Sydney). However, they seem to do better against West Indies, who will now provide the opposition in two of their last three preliminary games.

What of Botham, who was so hugely determined to finish his England touring with a big, big flourish? Since he made that memorable hundred in the Brisbane Test, the fact is he has played only one other innings of any note: a roaring 68 on New Year's Day, against Australia in a one-day affair in Perth. His medium pace bowling in this World Series Cup is looking pretty plain stuff. A topic, I fancy, for tomorrow's filing.

Awake this morning at 7 a.m., I find two messages under the bedroom door. One says: Could you please phone the London Telegraph? It was received by the Hilton at 11 p.m. last night. The second is a telex: 'Canst confirm urgentest for Monday's issue if report that Border returning Essexwards correct query ends Sportsed.' I don't doubt that Sportsed will think I have ignored both messages. I just mention them here to indicate how communications can be inadequate for one stupid reason or another and how relationships can become soured. Anyway, I at once ring the paper (it is still 8.30 p.m. GMT), explain why I have been silent so long and tell them I will check with Border soonest. I give Australia's captain another hour to wake up before telephoning his room. He confirms that he is not returning to Essex. I pass this on to London. 'Can you do a piece on it?' I am asked. It seems to me at this end to be one of those non-stories. 'What,' I enquire, 'can I say except that Border says he is not going back to Essex?' My point is taken. They will 'cobble something together' back home.

January 27

Last day in Adelaide, which we will be sorry to leave: an elegant, restful city superbly planned in the horse-and-buggy age by a Colonel William Light who must have had a vision of the wide streets needed in a future internal combustion era. It zealously preserves an inner ring of parks and gardens. It has been termed as 'possibly the last well-planned, well-governed and moderately contented metropolis on earth'.

BENSON AND HEDGES
WORLD SERIES CUP PRELIMINARY

26 January 1987

AUSTRALIA

G. R. Marsh	c Emburey b DeFreitas	8
D. M. Wellham	c Richards b DeFreitas	9
D. M. Jones	c Richards b DeFreitas	8
A. R. Border	c Broad b DeFreitas	91
S. R. Waugh	not out	83
S. P. O'Donnell	run out	6
G. R. J. Matthews	c Lamb b Dilley	0
T. J. Zoehrer	not out	5
Extras	(b 1, lb 8, w 4, nb 2)	12
TOTAL (for 6 wkts, 50 overs)		211

Did not bat: K. H. Macleay, P. L. Taylor, S. P. Davis.

Fall of wickets: 21, 24, 37, 201, 211, 219.

Bowling: Dilley 10-1-41-1; DeFreitas 10-1-35-4; Botham 10-0-42-0; Small 10-0-42-0; Emburey 10-0-56-0.

ENGLAND

B. C. Broad	c Border b Waugh	46
C. W. J. Athey	lbw b Davis	12
D. I. Gower	c Waugh b O'Donnell	21
M. W. Gatting	b Taylor	46
A. J. Lamb	run out	8
I. T. Botham	st Zoehrer b Taylor	18
C. J. Richards	b Waugh	2
J. E. Emburey	run out	17
P. A. J. DeFreitas	c Jones by Taylor	8
G. C. Small	b MacLeay	2
G. R. Dilley	not out	3
Extras	(lb 8, w 1)	9
TOTAL (48.1 overs)		192

Fall of wickets: 23, 55, 125, 138, 144, 152, 158, 184, 188.

Bowling: Davis 8-0-18-1; MacLeay 10-1-43-1; Matthews 4-0-21-0; O'Donnell 9-0-43-1; Waugh 10-1-30-2; Taylor 7.1-0-29-3.

Before we go, I have the nerve to impose on Sir Donald Bradman's privacy. When, back in December, he was kind enough to pay tribute to Walter Hammond for an HTV Bristol documentary, the photograph I had taken of the occasion turned out, along with a whole roll of film, to be a disaster. 'Dare I ask,' I enquire on the telephone, 'whether I can come out to your home this morning and take another?' 'Certainly,' he says. 'Can you be here at 11?'

So out we go, along with Dominic Allan, of Independent Radio News, and David Lloyd, of the Press Association, who are joining us for a trip to the South Australian vineyards. The great man welcomes us all at his front gate, and accommodates our every whim, including the signing of David's Wisden Book of Test Cricket, which is opened on the page reporting his last innings for Australia (0 at The Oval, in 1948). 'I think,' he says, with a glint in his eye, 'that I'd rather do it on a page where I got a few.' We all agree that his effort at Headingley in 1930 – 334 with 300 of them in one day – would be more appropriate.

I am very grateful, we all are very grateful, for the kindness and courtesy of a living legend. An equally generous Dominic and David give us a rather bibulous lunch, which we sleep off on a shore of the Great Australian Bight.

I file a piece about Ian Botham leaving things late if he is to finish his tour in the blaze of glory he envisaged, but have no great confidence that it will get into print. None of the wordage dispatched some days previously about the four unlucky players, and the future of Micky Stewart, got into print, in spite of the paper having five sports pages. Such things make the crosses reporters must patiently bear.

I would love to see I.B. going out on a batting high. I don't think there will be a bowling one now. He is still contributing his useful stint of ten medium paced overs to the pyjama games, though rather less effectively than was the case in the Perth Challenge. What he would enjoy more than anything else is a crash-bang hundred against West Indies.

January 28

That mean West Indian machine is creaking again, beaten this time by Australia in Sydney, by 36 runs. Australia 194, West Indies all out 158 in 46.1 overs. A crowd of 34,000 plus get their dollars' worth.

This result keeps Australia in the hunt to reach the finals and it will concentrate the minds of West Indies when they play England in Melbourne two days hence. If England can beat them again, they ought to qualify. They have the best run rate so far, and that will be a crucial factor if everyone finishes the prelims level on points.

Border's bold decision to go in first himself is no great success against some fast, extremely accurate and testing bowling. But from a modest 69 for 3 at the half-way stage Australia lift themselves to 150 for 4 with 10 overs to go. Subsequent activities are largely suicidal, Waugh, O'Donnell and Zoehrer all running themselves out.

West Indies, batting under the lights, ought to find themselves chasing something like 225. But the bounce is uneven, there is plenty of turn for the spinners, Australia bowl well and before too long it is apparent that if Viv Richards can't do the trick, no one else will. Taylor misses a testing catch in the deep when he has made 32, but Australia get their man for an imposing 70. Garner strikes two 6s, one of them a massive blow, but O'Donnell (man of the match) finishes with 4 for 19, Waugh with 2 for 21 and Matthews with 3 for 32.

January 30 (World Series Cup preliminary v. West Indies)

Back to Melbourne and another defeat for England, this time at the hands of West Indies by six wickets in a low-scoring game on a poor pitch. Not that it poses many problems for Viv Richards as a masterful 58 takes his side to the brink of victory. To think that he all but played on to Emburey, off the first ball he received.

England win the toss and have a big struggle from the

outset to make a modest 147 all out off 48.2 overs. Broad (33) holds the early batting together, Emburey (34) supervises later operations. The saddest incident involves Holding, who suffers a severely torn hamstring when taking a brave and brilliantly athletic return catch from Botham. He surely won't play again in this tournament. It might well mean the end of a great fast bowler's career.

Another 30-odd runs by England and they might have done the trick, even without Dilley, who seems constantly subject to minor stresses and strains. None the less, we see a rousing opening spell from DeFreitas and Small, and the early fall of Richardson. Haynes and Gomes, who usually gives some solidity to West Indies' batting, need a lot of luck to survive the rest of it. After Foster has had Haynes lbw, Richards takes watchful command and eventually launches his assault on Emburey. DeFreitas finishes with figures of 10-2-15-1. Small's final return of 10-3-16-0 is just as impressive. But England, beset by a number of niggling injuries, are looking jaded and not at all the buoyantly successful side they had been in the Perth Challenge.

This result throws the World Series Cup wide open again. All three countries are level, each of them with two more preliminary games to play. It must seem to England that these early games are going on for ever. They may yet pay the price for not beating Australia in Brisbane as well as in Adelaide, as they should have done.

January 31

No match and it's Saturday, so no paper to file for, and off to the beaches we go. I find the centre of Melbourne to be rather overpowering and oppressive, so it's a relief to drive down the freeway, past Geelong, where Prince Charles spent some of his formative time at school, to the recommended resort of Torquay. It has little in common with its English namesake and, having stupidly failed to take a

BENSON AND HEDGES
WORLD SERIES CUP PRELIMINARY

30 January 1987

ENGLAND

B. C. Broad	c Garner b Holding	33
C. W. J. Athey	lbw b Garner	2
D. I. Gower	b Marshall	8
A. J. Lamb	run out	0
M. W. Gatting*	b Harper	13
I. T. Botham	c&b Holding	15
J. E. Emburey	c Harper b Garner	34
P. A. J. DeFreitas	c Haynes b Garner	13
N. A. Foster	b Marshall	5
G. C. Small	not out	1
C. J. Richards†	b Marshall	8
Extras	(lb 3, w 4, nb 8)	15
TOTAL (all out, 48.2 overs)		147

Fall of wickets: 11, 27, 37, 61, 77, 84, 111, 136, 144.

Bowling: Marshall 9.2-2-30-3; Garner 9-1-37-3; Holding 8.3-2-19-2; Walsh 5-1-16-0; Harper 10-0-26-1; Richards 6.3-1-16-0.

WEST INDIES

D. L. Haynes	lbw b Foster	13
R. B. Richardson	c Richards b DeFreitas	0
L. Gomes	run out	36
I. V. A. Richards*	b Foster	58
A. L. Logie	not out	19
P. J. L. Dujon†	not out	1
Extras	(lb 10, w 8, nb 3)	21
TOTAL (for 4 wkts, 48.3 overs)		148

Did not bat: R. A. Harper, M. D. Marshall, M. A. Holding, J. Garner, C. A. Walsh.

Fall of wickets: 7, 49, 98, 146.

Bowling: DeFreitas 10-2-15-1; Small 10-3-16-0; Botham 10-3-28-0; Foster 9-1-25-2; Emburey 9.3-1-54-0.

picnic, we struggle to find an establishment which even sells fish and chips. But there is a lovely beach, just about visible amongst the teeming throng, the breezes blow some cobwebs away, and our companion, Peter Smith, gets burned by the sun.

I must not forget to record that the day began with the news, around 12.30 a.m., that Graham Dilley, after weeks of speculation, has decided to leave Kent and join Worcestershire. That makes another wee chore to be dealt with. The scribes are summoned to the manager's suite – Peter Lush, I imagine, not being best pleased to be kept awake at this hour – to hear Dilley's prepared statement which we think bears the stamp of Graham Otway, co-author of G.D.'s forthcoming book.

As a lifelong supporter of his old county, I am sorry Dilley feels he must move. He is entitled to make the best for himself, but I wonder if first-class cricket in England, with sponsors available to put up the big money, isn't moving to a sort of transfer system. It's a trend which the TCCB and the Cricketers' Association need to look at very carefully.

February 1 (World Series Cup preliminary v. Australia)

Another bad day for England in Melbourne: thrashed by Australia who make 248 for 5 after Gatting has put them in (no blame on the skipper for that), and then bowl out their opponents for 139, to win by 109 runs. It's a result which virtually assures Australia of a place in the final, and it leaves England to beat West Indies in Tasmania if they are to have any hope of joining them there.

The pitch plays rather better than it did the last time, but is far from being plumb. England's bowling overall is less than distinguished. Border makes 45, Jones 93 and Waugh a brilliant 49 not out. The last two have most to do with England being clattered for 84 in the last ten overs. Things no doubt would have been a good deal better if Botham had not put down a difficult catch off Border when the Australian skipper had made 10, and Jones, on 45, had been stumped off Gatting, as the TV replay clearly suggests he should have been.

Athey takes a fine catch and Lamb an astounding one, but Emburey gets hammered again and Gatting decides to bowl nine overs himself. This does nothing for the morale of Foster, who has sent down seven tidy overs in his first spell, but matters don't get out of hand until Waugh strikes the captain for 4 off the last three balls of a final over costing 16.

Just who he should bowl is not the least of Gatting's problems. He has to field a long way from the wicket to protect those in his side with suspect throwing arms. There is a fearful din from a crowd of almost 59,000. He looks like a bookmaker making tic-tac signals.

England's batsmen are never in the chase when their turn comes, even though Botham goes in first. He struggles to make 45 off 26 overs. Gower gets out to a lazy pull shot, Gatting to one for which he is never in position, and Lamb, would you believe it, is run out for the third time in successive innings – not once, so far as I can see, through his own fault. The odds against that happening must be pretty short.

I thought Lamb's catch was a terrific effort, but so is the return one taken by Matthews to end Botham's innings. Any man standing in the firing line of a full-blooded smash from Botham deserves a medal. He takes another pretty spectacular one at deep mid-wicket to end England's wholly inadequate reply. He may be a bit of a rum extrovert but, my word, he *can* catch. And bowl, too, in these affairs. Whereas in three Test Matches he had 2 for 295, he has now taken 7 for 174 in this tournament in about 52 overs. Emburey in his last three outings has had 0 for 151 at six an over. I don't think this proves anything, but it does indicate that the Test game and the pyjama game are as different as chalk and cheese.

BENSON AND HEDGES
WORLD SERIES CUP PRELIMINARY

1 February 1987

AUSTRALIA

G. R. Marsh	c Emburey b Foster	28
A. R. Border*	c Athey b Small	45
D. M. Jones	c Athey b Gatting	93
G. M. Ritchie	st French b Gatting	9
D. M. Wellham	c Lamb b Gatting	3
S. R. Waugh	not out	49
S. O'Donnell	not out	4
Extras	(lb 7, w 9, nb 1)	17
TOTAL (for 5 wkts, 50 overs)		248

Did not bat: G. R. J. Matthews, T. J.Zoehrer, P. L. Taylor, S. P. Davis.

Fall of wickets: 61, 127, 144, 154, 223.

Bowling: DeFreitas 8-2-37-0; Small 10-0-49-1; Botham 10-0-35-0; Foster 7-1-20-1; Emburey 6-0-41-0; Gatting 9-0-59-3.

ENGLAND

B. C. Broad	b O'Donnell	2
I. T. Botham	c&b Matthews	45
D. I. Gower	c Taylor b Davis	11
A. J. Lamb	run out	11
M. W. Gatting*	c Davis b Waugh	6
C. W. J. Athey	lbw b O'Donnell	29
J. E. Emburey	b Matthews	1
P. A. J. DeFreitas	b Waugh	11
N. A. Foster	b Waugh	4
B. N. French†	not out	5
G. C. Small	c Matthews b Jones	4
Extras	(b 2, lb 7, w 1)	10
TOTAL (all out, 47.3 overs)		139

Fall of wickets: 4, 25, 52, 65, 87, 90, 117, 129, 130.

Bowling: Davis 8-1-20-1; O'Donnell 9-2-33-2; Matthews 10-1-24-2; Waugh 10-0-26-3, Taylor 9-1-23-0; Jones 1.3-0-4-1.

158

February 2

Across the Bass Strait to Devonport, for our final preliminary, against West Indies, in a game none of us is optimistic
about winning. I don't doubt that management is prudent
to make contingency plans for an earlier flight home.

Devonport stands at the mouth of the Mersey river at the
centre of Tasmania's north coast: a neat and pleasant town,
the gateway to some of the island's wildest and most
beautiful scenery. A fine cricket Oval, its facilities considerably superior to those we saw in Hobart, is within yards of
the sea.

February 3 (World Series Cup preliminary v. West Indies)

We are celebrating this evening another remarkable and
surprising victory, and reflecting, by no means for the first
time, what a funny old game this cricket can be. England,
put in first on a lively pitch of bounce and movement, make
177 for 9 wickets, thanks very largely to a skilful, disciplined 76 from Broad, and then bowl out West Indies for
148 to win by 29 runs. I was craven enough to think that on
such a pitch Dilley, who is still nursing one of his frequent
niggling injuries, would be sadly missed. But England's
bowlers come up trumps, Gatting's bowling changes are
made to look positively inspired, and some fine catches are
taken.

Plans for early departure are swiftly and quietly shelved.
This result – after all had seemed lost – puts England
through to the best of three games final against Australia.
They have now beaten West Indies four times in five
encounters – after having won only five of the previous 22.
It is the first time in five World Series Cup tournaments that
West Indies have failed to make the last round. Are they on
the slide at last? That's something to write about tomorrow,
perhaps.

Back now to today's success, which should give
England's jaded side just the uplift they need for a grand-

stand finish. Mike Gatting admits afterwards that they haven't played well against Australia, but hopes now that they can give everyone back home something more to celebrate. After this reprieve, I feel in my ageing bones that they might very well do just that.

Gatting also admits that England would have made less than 100 without Broad, who holds the fort for more than three hours and duly takes the man of the match award. Lamb helps him to shore up the middle of the innings with an invaluable 36, and DeFreitas makes a handy 15 not out towards the end. Botham gets a nasty lifter in what I then supposed must be his last innings for England overseas.

Greenidge and Haynes are missing from the West Indies batting and England get the early wickets they badly need. But the decisive breakthrough comes in mid-innings when West Indies are reduced from 71 for 2 to 95 for 6. By then Botham, who had the makeshift opener Payne with his first ball, has 3 for 33, the others being Gomes and – most precious scalp of all – Richards, who nicks an off-cutter on to his stumps. Foster and Small oblige their captain with a wicket apiece when recalled for a second spell.

England are in the box seat now – or are they? Dujon and Marshall, who looks dangerous, rattle up 37 off 7 overs to supply another twist. 132 for 6 in the 43rd, another 46 required: that makes it a different game entirely. This is the point when DeFreitas, who has bowled magnificently in this tournament, roars back with the wicket of Marshall in the first over of his second spell. This is the second decisive moment. England have tight control now, West Indies falling further behind the clock, and Emburey, returning to the attack for his ninth over, contrives two wickets off the first two balls (both from full tosses) and bowls the heaving Garner with the last.

There has been a lot of pressure today on all of England's bowlers, not least on Foster, who has not had much of a tour. He has come good on this occasion, he bowled well against Australia two days ago in Melbourne, and, even if Dilley declares himself fit again, the selectors would need to think very hard before leaving Foster out of the first game in the final.

February 4

England have pitched camp again in Melbourne, after thinking they would be taking temporary tents to Sydney before flying home, and West Indies, looking down in the mouth, have flown out of Devonport en route for a last pre-liminary game, against Australia, which becomes a token contest. Even if they win it, they have to bat first and score 374 to edge above England's run rate. 'I'm a man of faith,' Viv Richards has said, 'but that's beyond us.'

West Indies' middle batting is looking fragile these days, more depending on the mighty Richards than it ought to do, but suggestions about a decline in their powers must be tempered by the fact that one-day restrictions here draw the teeth of their attack. They have also had a lot of injuries.

February 5

I really ought not to have suggested to my readers that Michael Holding's distinguished career seemed at an end after that mishap he had last week. He has made an astonishing recovery from his hamstring tear and – surprise, surprise – he is in the West Indian team, announced today, which will shortly tour New Zealand. So is Gordon Greenidge, who also passed a fitness test on a hamstring last evening. Greenidge's inclusion is as much of a surprise. He hasn't played in their last four games and rumour has it that his management, running out of patience, were not at all prepared to endorse his selection for another tour. Rumour also suggests that it is Richards' influence which has kept him in the side. Their batting certainly needs the old firm of Haynes and Greenidge to give it a decent start.

BENSON AND HEDGES
WORLD SERIES CUP PRELIMINARY

3 February 1987

ENGLAND

B. C. Broad	c Dujon b Walsh	76
I. T. Botham	c Richardson b Gray	8
D. I. Gower	c Payne b Marshall	3
A. J. Lamb	c Logie b Harper	36
M. W. Gatting*	c Richardson b Gray	6
C. W. J. Athey	lbw b Marshall	3
J. E. Emburey	c Garner b Walsh	2
P. A. J. DeFreitas	not out	15
N. A. Foster	run out	0
B. N. French†	b Marshall	0
G. C. Small	not out	6
Extras	(lb 14, w 3, nb 5)	22
TOTAL (for 9 wkts, 50 overs)		177

Fall of wickets: 24, 29, 103, 129, 133, 143, 158, 159, 160.

Bowling: Marshall 10-0-31-3; Gray 10-2-29-2; Garner 10-0-30-0; Walsh 10-1-31-2; Harper 10-0-42-1.

WEST INDIES

R. B. Richardson	c French b DeFreitas	2
T. R. O. Payne	c French b Botham	18
A. L. Logie	b Foster	31
H. A. Gomes	c Emburey b Botham	19
I. V. A. Richards	b Botham	1
P. L. J. Dujon	c Gatting b Emburey	34
R. A. Harper	c French b Small	4
M. Marshall	c Athey b DeFreitas	27
J. Garner	b Emburey	4
A. H. Gray	c&b Emburey	0
C. A. Walsh	not out	1
Extras	(lb 5, w 2)	7
TOTAL (48 overs)		148

Fall of wickets: 10, 25, 71, 73, 90, 95, 132, 147, 147, 148.

Bowling: DeFreitas 9-1-20-2; Small 10-0-35-1; Foster 10-0-29-1; Botham 10-1-33-3; Emburey 9-0-26-3.

Roger Harper, magnificent fielder though he is, apparently had an indifferent tour of Pakistan before coming to Australia, and he has now made way for another off-spinner, Clyde Butts, who did well in Pakistan. Harper, though considered an all-rounder, has made few runs in recent games here. The other new man for the tour is Carl Hooper, from Guyana, who replaces Winston Benjamin. Hooper is only 21 and, by all accounts, a batsman of rare potential. I am told that he broke all records for Werneth in the Lancashire League last summer.

February 6

A reprieved England side have nets at 'MCG' – their first full session, as it happens, since before the start of the Perth Challenge some five weeks ago. I do not agree with criticism that they have not practised assiduously enough in that time, although some kind of concerted physical activity would not have come amiss. I think Micky Stewart and the captain, looking at the state of affairs day by day, were realistic in believing that, as the number of niggling injuries increased, nets on non-playing days would have been an unproductive chore for a side jaded in mental and physical terms. They still had several full sessions on the mornings of day/night games. It should also be remembered that the onus of playing all the big encounters has fallen virtually on only twelve players. Bruce French and Neil Foster have had a welcome opportunity in the last two affairs, and James Whitaker had one, a long time ago now, in the Adelaide Test.

England have two major injury problems before the Cup final: Chris Broad with a hamstring made no better by his match-winning innings in Devonport, and Graham Dilley, with a shoulder problem which permits him to bowl but affects his throwing arm. It's a comfort to see Broad batting today without notable discomfort. Dilley, who bowls in the nets at a relatively gentle pace, will have a fitness test tomorrow morning before England pick their squad. Provided that he can convince both himself and his selectors that he is capable of delivering the goods, Dilley, as principal strike bowler this Australian summer, should get the vote. I imagine England will go in with four seam bowlers at Melbourne, so who to leave out? Gladstone Small, who has had a mild virus complaint of late, has not been quite so accurate in recent games. Neil Foster, late to the post, has come up trumps. It could be a close decision.

Micky Stewart leads the scribes to suppose that Ian Botham may open the innings again, with Bill Athey going in at No. 3 in the event of early trouble, or lower down as the case may be. There is no question of omitting Athey, whose fielding and catching on the leg side are highly regarded. He has anyway made more runs in this competition than any other England batsman save Broad. It is high time that one or two others, notably Gower and Gatting, kept their heads down longer.

Stewart says that for England to have reached the final represents a 100 per cent effort in his book – 'to win at Devonport was a performance of guts and character' – and for them to win, it would be something more. 'I'm certain the lads are fired up for a grandstand finish,' he adds. They ought to be. They can pull off a remarkable treble now.

One unhappy hiccough today: Botham gets rapped on a thumb by a ball of medium pace from Phillip DeFreitas, hurls his bat down and utters an expletive not calculated to charm several women and young children behind the net. He declines, in spite of a later invitation from his captain, to participate in fielding practice but joins some other players in bowling at Elton John. Several of my colleagues get steamed up about what they regard as a frivolous activity – which indeed it is, since Mr John's technique does not match up to his obvious enthusiasm for the game. But it seems to me to be a harmless exercise. The England nets had been officially declared closed.

Quite an exciting climax to the last preliminary game

between Australia and West Indies at Sydney, the result of which can have no bearing on the line-up for the final. That doesn't deter more than 32,000 spectators from turning up at SCG to see Australia win under the floodlights by 2 wickets with 5 balls left.

West Indies are without Greenidge, Haynes, Marshall and Holding, all of them injured. When they win the toss and bat first, the stopgap opener, Thelston Payne, left hander and reserve wicketkeeper, is soon added to the casualty list with yet another of the hamstring tears which seem to bedevil cricketers these days, but he makes top score, 60, in a total of 192 on a slow pitch. Richards, just when he is looking threatening, falls for 25 to another of Matthews's spectacular return catches. But the most news-worthy item in the innings is the reprieve of a batsman who has been given out for obstructing the field.

Benjamin pushes a ball from Taylor back down the pitch. Gray, backing up too enthusiastically, and knowing what his fate will be, sticks out his bat to deflect the ball out of Taylor's grasp. He has to be out, to a dismissal very rarely seen. Umpire's finger raised. Gray trudges off. But with a nice, if quixotic, gesture Border pleads with the umpire that the batsman be recalled. I doubt if he would have done that had the scores been level, the last pair together, but it is cer-tainly a handsome thing to do, and it ought to spare the Australian captain too many 'throat' balls when next he faces Gray in another capacity.

Border sends in Zoehrer to open with Marsh, with instantly happy results. Zoehrer's antics behind the stumps, and his incessant appealing, have not endeared him to his opponents, but they know he can bat a bit. He now strikes 50, off only 59 balls, out of 74 for the first Australian wicket. From such a firm base, his side ought to cruise home – as indeed, thanks to O'Donnell, they finally do. But at one point they are 165 for 6, with 5 overs left, and another 28 needed. No cause for panic stations. O'Donnell takes 19 off 14 balls, and 4 off his next to win the game. It doesn't matter that Border and Matthews are bowled by Richards in the 49th over. By then, I am sure, Richards has settled for another defeat, the seventh suffered by West Indies in eleven limited overs games since December 30. For Australia it is now four wins in a row. They are still going well with an unchanged side, but I doubt if they will go into the final without Reid.

February 7

I ought during the course of this tour to have chronicled the progress – or the lack of it – made by Sportsed in his search for a successor to Michael Carey as a full-time cricket correspondent. I am reminded to do so now by rumours that yet another candidate is in the frame.

I believe the post was first offered to Peter Smith of the *Daily Mail*, then to Matthew Engel of *The Guardian* and, after he, too, had declined it, to Scyld Berry of *The Observer*. Matthew, a writer of brilliant talent, knows that his gifts are far better suited to his present journal, and so does Scyld, who I dare say prefers the less onerous duties of serving a Sunday paper.

We next heard strong rumours that the *Telegraph* job had been offered to Martin Johnson, of *The Independent*, another gifted writer but one not thought too willing to leap at this new opportunity. Martin may well have remained the front runner at the time he returned home after the final Test. However, we assumed he had turned the offer down when hearing that Alan Lee had become the next name in line. Alan, a most capable and professional journalist, came out here to finish his time with the *Mail on Sunday* before returning to England to take up a new post with *Sports-Week*.

I am now reminded to mention this drawn-out saga by word from home that a freelance, Mihir Bose, was recently thought to be the latest favoured candidate. Then we heard that another approach had been made to Peter Smith. The list, which does not include the names of several journalists who in my judgement would be right for the job, is long and diverse enough to suggest that Sportsed has no clear idea what sort of a reporter his paper needs.

February 8 (first World Series Cup final v. Australia)

Ian Botham has been due, indeed overdue, for at least one last fling and, my word, he enjoys it today in the first of the final games. Going in first and making the most of the local regulation that, for the first fifteen overs of an innings, seven fielders must be within the two semi-circular lines, he launches such a daring and brutal assault as to make England's subsequent victory by six wickets a virtual formality. Receiving 52 balls, he strikes 71 out of 91 for the first wicket in something less than 15 overs with a 6 and eleven 4s. Broad, his share in the opening partnership a modest dozen, is quite happy to play second fiddle.

After Botham departs to a catch at long off – and to a fervent ovation – it is good to see Athey coming in next: an indication that England intend to keep their heads down. As it happens he goes, after making 12, to as spectacular a return catch by Matthews as the one taken by Jones at extra cover to end Broad's innings for a similar score. But Gower plays quite beautifully for 45 and, this being the time for celebration and charity, I will not go into harrowing detail about his last stroke. England simply coast home.

I am surprised to hear afterwards that Border would have batted first had he won the toss. Whereas the temperature in Melbourne yesterday had been 104 degrees, today in a city of unpredictable climatic changes it is cool and grey. Damp, too, first thing. The start is delayed and the overs reduced to 44, which just shows how Channel 9 is determined to have its finish at the advertised time. Several hours of daylight remain after it is all over. More than 51,000 spectators get less than their money's worth.

Zoehrer may have done the trick as an opener for Australia

against West Indies, but he fails now, a victim of Dilley's swing in the first over of the day. Gatting takes another slip catch to get rid of Marsh in the first one sent down by DeFreitas. Then a threatening partnership, 103 in 26 overs, by Jones and Border, and England lament a missed chance when Jones has made 36. My heart bleeds for Whitaker, who is substituting briefly. He gets under a steepler off Botham but puts it down.

Foster ends the stand by having Border taken behind and Australia, still quite well placed for a decent total, make a porridge of the final run-in against some tight outcricket. The impetuous Jones runs out Ritchie, Dilley's throwing arm being equal to the test, Waugh holes out off Emburey to a catch by DeFreitas who then has Jones playing on for 67. Australia total 171 for 8. Dilley has 3 for 32, DeFreitas 2 for the same number and Foster's return, 9-0-42-1, does him scant justice. Note, too, that Botham has bowled 9 accurate overs for only 26. Good bowling again, all round.

February 9

Is this the last time we will be seeing Sydney on this trip? It will be if we win again in two days' time. The lads are riding high again, the old buoyant mood recaptured. The squad will be announced after nets tomorrow. Thirteen again, I imagine, Edmonds probably replacing Foster, and French, who has looked very sharp behind the stumps, remaining in a winning combination.

Australia are sticking by the same twelve. Next time, they ought to restore a batsman, Wellham, and omit a bowler, probably Reid or Davis. They ought to open with Border again, and I can't see them playing without two spinners on what these days is just about their only happy hunting ground. Matthews, quite apart from his remarkable catches, has taken 8 wickets for 83 in his last three games – off only 27.1 overs.

FIRST BENSON AND HEDGES
WORLD SERIES CUP FINAL

8 February 1987

AUSTRALIA

G. R. Marsh	c Gatting b DeFreitas	2
T. J. Zoehrer†	c Gatting b DeFreitas	0
D. M. Jones	b DeFreitas	67
A. R. Border*	c French b Foster	42
G. M. Ritchie	run out	13
S. R. Waugh	c DeFreitas b Emburey	1
S. P. O'Donnell	b Dilley	10
G. R. J. Matthews	b Dilley	8
P. L. Taylor	not out	3
B. A. Reid	not out	5
Extras	(lb 10, w 3, nb 7)	20
TOTAL (for 8 wkts)		171

Did not bat: S. P. Davis.

Fall of wickets: 3, 3, 106, 134, 137, 146, 161, 164.

Bowling: Dilley 9-2-32-2; DeFreitas 9-0-32-2; Botham 9-0-26-0; Foster 9-0-42-1; Emburey 8-0-29-1.

ENGLAND

B. C. Broad	c Jones b Matthews	12
I. T. Botham	c Marsh b Matthews	71
C. W. J. Athey	c&b Matthews	12
D. I. Gower	c Taylor b Reid	45
A. J. Lamb	not out	15
M. W. Gatting*	not out	3
Extras	(lb 3, b 5, w 4, nb 2)	14
TOTAL (for 4 wkts)		172

Did not bat: J. E. Emburey, P. A. J. DeFreitas, N. A. Foster, B. N. French, G. R. Dilley.

Fall of wickets: 91, 93, 147, 159.

Bowling: Davis 4-0-17-0; O'Donnell 4-0-25-0; Reid 5-0-31-1; Waugh 8-1-36-0; Matthews 9-1-27-3; Taylor 5-0-24-0; Jones 1-0-4-0.

Clive Lloyd, who has been out here for some while, has announced his retirement from the game. A great player, a lovely, avuncular man and an immensely successful Test captain – but, in my book, a cynical one who played his intimidatory cards to the very limit allowed by law or too indulgent umpires.

February 10

Chris Broad has deservedly won the Benson and Hedges International Cricketer of the Year award, which has previously gone to Viv Richards (on three occasions), Dennis Lillee, Bruce Yardley, David Gower and Richard Hadlee. Not bad going for a player not in England's frame six months ago. It couldn't happen to a nicer, more level-headed man.

Thanks to the initiative and organisational flair of *The Guardian's* Matthew Engel, we all enjoy an end-of-tour press dinner with our Australian colleagues at the Mixing Pot restaurant. We have spent a great deal of time in each others' company these last four months, and this is the last chance for purely social enjoyment. Mike Coward (*Sydney Morning Herald*) and Matthew make brief and felicitous speeches on behalf of both teams, Mike alluding to the fact that Ross Mullins, of Australian Associated Press, has just completed 50 years in sports journalism. Ross is a doyen indeed, a great old pro and always great fun to work with.

February 11 (second World Series Cup final v. Australia)

England, by just 8 runs! The Cup is theirs, for overflowing, in two straight games. We all breathe again, not least the manager who more than once during the afternoon and evening must have been on the point of further adjustment to hotel and travel arrangements.

It has been another typical limited overs finish, one to

twist the gut. A brave innings by O'Donnell, twice lofting DeFreitas for 6 with some glorious strokes, brings Australia, 8 wickets down, to within 18 runs of victory when Foster bowls the last over.

Foster's first 4 overs, earlier in the evening, have gone for 20, and his skipper takes him off. His next five, mid-innings, yield 21 – no shame in that – and he is rested again. But, now, Dilley and DeFreitas have finished their ration, and Foster is under a good deal of pressure. He remembers, we all remember, what Lamb so startlingly achieved here three weeks ago. To his lasting credit, he sends down a very good over, Taylor taking a single off the first ball and O'Donnell managing only four 2s off the next 5. England's joy is unconfined. A clean sweep in all three competitions they have played. Three days off at Bondi Junction. No need to return to Melbourne. An arduous tour ends on the finest possible note. Those who inhabit the press box, of whatever persuasion, share England's relief.

The morning is cool and grey, with rain in the offing. England leave out Edmonds, Australia restore Wellham for Reid. Gatting wins the toss. This Sydney pitch can never be taken for granted but we wonder, when England have made 187 for 9, whether it is quite enough. For that total we are greatly obliged to Botham for another blistering start – 25 out of 31 off less than 8 overs – to the ever trustworthy Broad for a 53 which holds the piece together until the 33rd over, and to Lamb, whose quite invaluable 35, made without risk in the later stages off 39 balls, ensures that the bowlers have a target at their backs.

Ritchie and O'Donnell take exciting catches to dispose of Botham and Broad, both of them off fine shots not quite kept down. Gower makes 17 with consummate ease before departing to a flaccid stroke. Gatting, to his surprise, is adjudged run out for 6. Matthews and Taylor each take 2 wickets for 30-odd.

What price England when Marsh and Border, living dangerously against the early bowling, raise 55 for the first wicket by the 19th over? It is Botham who does the trick again, with the wickets of both openers, as well as that of Ritchie, for 7 runs off 27 balls – after which there can be no question that he will be named player of the finals. More importantly, no doubt, Emburey takes another of his marvellous catches, a return one from Jones, as he dives far to his left. Jones gone for 13, a danger man removed.

Australia are 80 for 4 now: a different ball-game altogether. But Waugh is run out by Foster (he looks 'in' on the replay, but that may be justice for Wellham being given 'in' when he seems run out by Small). When DeFreitas roars back to have Wellham (30) and Zoehrer with consecutive balls, it is 135 for 7 and Australia soon need 50 off the last 5.

In the end, we rejoice that England's outcricket has delivered the goods again. Dilley 10-1-34-0; DeFreitas 10-1-34-2; Botham 10-1-26-3; Emburey (one of his most restrictive stints) 10-2-27-1; and, yes, Foster, too with 10-0-51-0.

The team have won themselves another 32,000 Australian dollars in prize money, bringing the total kitty from such sources in the various competitions to about £70,000.

February 12

None of this, I gather, needs to be spent at an all-night party, hosted by Elton John to celebrate what has been achieved. Dennis Lillee misses part of it through getting stuck in a lift at the team's apartment block which looks out over Bondi beach. It is reported that the police and the fire brigade have been sent for to iron out certain local difficulties.

At his last media conference Mike Gatting, quaffing orange juice, flourishes a nice, congratulatory cable just received from Mrs Thatcher. There had been nothing similar after victory in the Test series, the Ashes retained, but Downing Street has got it right this time.

SECOND BENSON AND HEDGES WORLD SERIES CUP FINAL

11 February 1987

ENGLAND

B. C. Broad	c O'Donnell b Matthews	53
I. T. Botham	c Ritchie b O'Donnell	25
C. W. J. Athey	b Matthews	16
D. I. Gower	c Wellham b Taylor	17
M. W. Gatting*	run out	7
A. J. Lamb	c Zoehrer b O'Donnell	35
J. E. Emburey	c Zoehrer b Waugh	6
P. A. J. DeFreitas	c Jones b Taylor	1
N. A. Foster	c Taylor b Davis	7
B. N. French†	not out	9
G. R. Dilley	not out	6
Extras	(lb 4, w 1)	5
TOTAL (for 9 wkts, 50 overs)		187

Fall of wickets: 36, 73, 102, 120, 121, 143, 146, 170, 170.

Bowling: Davis 10-0-44-1; O'Donnell 10-1-37-2; Waugh 10-0-42-1; Matthews 10-1-31-2; Taylor 10-2-29-2.

AUSTRALIA

G. R. Marsh	lbw b Botham	28
A. R. Border*	c French b Botham	27
D. M. Jones	c&b Emburey	13
G. M. Ritchie	c DeFreitas b Botham	4
D. M. Wellham	c Gower b DeFreitas	30
S. R. Waugh	run out	22
S. P. O'Donnell	not out	40
T. J. Zoehrer†	lbw b DeFreitas	0
G. R. J. Matthews	run out	3
P. L. Taylor	not out	3
Extras	(b 1, lb 6, w 2)	9
TOTAL (for 8 wkts, 50 overs)		179

Did not bat: S. P. Davis.

Fall of wickets: 55, 70, 72, 80, 124, 135, 135, 151.

Bowling: Dilley 10-1-34-0; DeFreitas 10-1-34-2; Botham 10-1-26-3; Foster 10-0-51-0; Emburey 10-2-27-1.

We don't expect England's captain to say anything that will have the wires humming, and he doesn't. He reiterates that it has been a happy tour. 'I think the word "happy" is important,' he says. It is, and for that he deserves much of the credit. Peter Lush confirms that his official report will include recommendations for less arduous touring in future years. Nothing can now be done about England's schedule for 1987/88: World Cup in India and Pakistan, a tour of Pakistan, a tour of New Zealand not to mention bicentennial matches in Australia. All that may seem like a marathon course.

John Emburey will be staying on a while in Melbourne with his Australian wife, Susie, and their two young children. Gladstone Small is off to join his Australian fiancée, Lois, in Adelaide. Ian Botham and Allan Lamb are remaining pro tem in Australia. Phil and Frances Edmonds propose, as we do, to fossick for a few days on the coral strand at Hamilton Island, close to the Great Barrier Reef. David Gower will be stopping off in Singapore. The rest of the party fly home from Sydney in three days' time – to what ought to be a rousing welcome.

I now reflect on the sixteen players who have shared a memorable experience and written their piece of cricket history.

At the head of the class, Mike Gatting, a good tactician, a positive, uncomplicated skipper who has earned the respect of his own side and that of his opponents. He has led from the front, setting a lively example in the field, holding some fine catches and enjoying a good Test series with the bat. Had less success in the pyjama game, getting himself out too often to impatient shots. So long as he goes on winning, he can be as dull as he likes at media conferences.

England's Admirable Crichton and vice-captain, John Emburey, has had a splendid all-round tour: a knowing, calm and flexible cricketer with the happy knack of doing what seems to be required. Forget a few of his one-day figures: he had 18 wickets in the Tests, often got invaluable runs, held some stunning catches and always brought a shrewd mind to every situation.

Bill Athey is another canny operator who plays like the old pros used to do. England despaired of getting a decent start when the First Test was played. No specialist opener, he made a quite crucial contribution to that thrilling Brisbane victory by batting right through a fraught first day for 76. To his success with the bat he has added his skills as fielder and catcher close in: an important contribution to the outcricket.

Ian Botham's last England tour, frustrated in midstream by injury, did not consistently go as he planned it, but it began and finished on a stirring note. It is no coincidence that his most effective efforts in the Test series, a stupendous 138 in Brisbane, and 5 first innings wickets in Melbourne, played a telling part in the matches England won. He remains the biggest drawcard in the game, a potential matchwinner as batsman or as slip catcher, and a bowler, even at reduced pace, still not to be taken lightly.

For a batsman who had scarcely been in England's Test Match reckoning for more than two years, Chris Broad, international cricketer of this year, has had a wonderfully consistent tour, making 1,046 runs in all the big encounters. He always plays very straight. He has a fine temperament, makes the most of his reach and, now, is a much more accomplished player on the off side. He has been another to cling on to some exciting catches.

I have previously remarked that Australia, for all their present troubles, are lucky to have young players of the calibre of Jones and Waugh. England now certainly have one, even younger, in Phillip DeFreitas, who will be 21 in a few days' time. The advance of this very exciting cricketer has been astonishing. He began his Test career with a bang, faced difficulties in mid-series and finished his tour with some consistently fiery and accurate bowling. He is a thrilling fielder, with an enviable arm. He should make many runs in time for his country. A natural competitor, with an instinctive 'feel'. Unselfish, and still wears the same size hat.

Graham Dilley's potential has been long apparent. On this tour he consistently proved himself as a strike bowler of genuine quality. He was quick, he was accurate and he swung the ball away from the right handers when conditions were helpful. He not only did a fine job for England in the Test series, often on unhelpful pitches, but in the abbreviated game as well, when he and DeFreitas were the best opening pair in the business, including that of West Indies.

One of the best things about the Test series was to see England sticking by a balanced attack throughout. Phil Edmonds bowled consistently well, not the least of his value being his ability to get Border out and to contain the aggressively minded Jones. He acquired some useful, pragmatic runs from time to time but is not quite so athletic a fielder as he used to be. He still remains a good, versatile one. His attitude to being left out of the side quite often in one-day games remains of the *que sera sera* variety.

Neil Foster did not bowl accurately enough in the early part of the tour to be a strong contender for the Test side. His enthusiasm and determination remained unimpaired, and it was good to see him taking his chance well towards the climax of the World Series Cup. He had two very good matches, then a more testing final one in which, at the end of it, he bowled a very important last over without losing his nerve.

Bruce French has been one of the unlucky ones, losing his Test place to Jack Richards, falling ill in December but making the most of his chances at the end of the tour after Jack's batting had lost its gloss. For all his disappointment, his attitude was always professional and cheerful, and he remains a very polished keeper.

The manner in which David Gower so often got himself out on this tour drove his supporters – and I dare say himself – to near-despair. His form and attitude have to be measured against a background in which he had lost the captaincy of England – as well, later, as that of Leicester-shire – and, initially, had not been invited to act as a team selector out here. He still scored more than 400 Test runs. No one could fault his charm, his friendliness and outward good cheer, or his loyalty to his captain.

Allan Lamb must know that his Test Match place is under threat: he had a disappointing series, and admits that, never feeling out of form, he sometimes was in too much of a hurry. However, his batting in the one day affairs made a vital contribution to England's success – and that in spite of the fact that he was run out in three consecutive innings. He is still an excellent fielder, and his influence on general morale remains irrepressible.

In purely physical terms, not to mention the consistent mental pressures, Jack Richards had the most demanding tour of anybody. From November, he played in every game, including four Tests, two State matches and ten pyjama flurries, without a break. When his batting, naturally enough, went off the boil, he surrendered the gloves to French. But he can look back with pride on a fine Test hundred, some very useful runs on other occasions, and some uplifting catches.

I have felt very sorry for Wilfred Slack, whose early form with the bat had him ruled out of consideration for the Test side. By mid-December he was batting serenely in two State matches, but by then the tour had simply passed him by. He is a delightful man with a most equable temperament. I fear his England days are done.

There was no more popular or likeable member of the side than Gladstone Small, who waited a long time for his big breakthrough and certainly made the most of it by winning the man of the match award in the Melbourne Test. What's more, he again took 5 wickets in an innings in Sydney. A reliable, consistent, accurate performer. He lost his edge a little towards the end, when Foster got his break.

Another member of the party who had to exercise his patience was James Whitaker, though he got his chance – and fluffed it – in the Third Test when Botham was injured.

He played his last innings – let alone a one-day outing – on December 20. It was tough for an ambitious young cricketer to have to wait so long in the wings, but another chance may come soon, in Sharjah for a start. I admire his level head and his very sensible attitude. A nice lad.

February 17

We have spent several days relaxing in Sydney with Diana Fisher, a most generous hostess who always finds time to welcome old friends and new ones in spite of the dizzy pace at which she conducts her life in television, radio and journalism. Not every lady can claim to have been married by an Archbishop of Canterbury to one of his sons, Humphrey, in Lambeth Palace. Humphrey is one of my oldest and most respected friends in BBC television. He has recently retired, the last twenty-odd years of his working life having been spent with the Australian Broadcasting Commission.

I am writing these final paragraphs, I might say courtesy of Henry Blofeld, from Hamilton Island, which is close to the Great Barrier Reef. It was Henry's suggestion that we should spend a week at a resort which I can only describe as the nearest thing to a tropical paradise that I have ever envisaged. The setting is stunningly beautiful. The facilities provide for every taste, athletic or indolent. Mine, of the latter variety, could hardly be better catered for as I laze hard by a swimming pool with a water temperature in the upper 80s F, and a buggy, known as the Boozemobile, brings regular refreshment to our side.

Henry is bound today for New Zealand, there to cover the West Indian tour. Phil and Frances Edmonds are staying on a while, Frances still having her diary to complete. I think she is a charmer, and we have greatly enjoyed their company.

We have just seen pictures on television of Mike Gatting and his braves arriving home on a bitterly cold morning at Heathrow. A world away, and the harsher realities of life soon to be unfolded for more of us.